Parents, it's time to R.E.S.E.T.

How to rescue YOURSELF and lead your CHILDREN to their GREATNESS

By: Willie Lee Tubbs

Praises for
"Parents, it's time to R.E.S.E.T."

"From the introduction chapter, I knew 'the story is with him.' Willie catches your attention immediately with a powerful story that has stuck with him all through life. His ability to weave in his story and experiences creates an attention-binding read. You sit on the edge of your seat in anticipation for what real-life experience he might share next. Add to his story-telling experience the powerful life lessons he has learned along his journey, he uses easy-to-remember acronyms to anchor those lessons in your mind. Willie certainly delivers on the promise to give the reader six tips from real-world experience that can allow any parent who implements them to move toward being a world-class parent. This book can serve as an excellent guide for parents who want to raise their children to achieve their potential."

–Dean Renfro,
Amazon Best Selling Author
and Certified Speaker, Coach,
and Trainer with the John Maxwell Team

"*Parents, it's time to R.E.S.E.T.* is a must-read. This book has touched my heart in so many ways. Growing up without a father, for me, was indeed difficult. Countless times I had to discover God's plans for my own life. As a man, father, husband, and soldier, I had to unlearn to learn. This book is not only inspirational but conformational as well. The author reveals simple solutions to complex problems we face as parents. One example is D.R.E.A.M., which is a biblically-based approach to allowing God to direct your steps. To find out what I mean, you must get your copy of this amazing book."

–Ray Wiley (Sheep Dog),
Veteran, Police Officer

"From start to finish, this book is a perfect example of how to reset your mind as a father and take control of your children for the future. It starts by being a wonderful loving father in any household. And the great thing about this book is, it will teach you values on why a great parent can lead to great children for a better future. Every guy, young or old, with or without children, should read this book for guidance."

–Lem Moore,
Marketing Expert, and Speaker

"The expectation was already high, but what I did not expect written within the pages of these chapters was a blueprint for success in life, love, and legacy. Willie's journey will undoubtedly give you the keys to unlock your inner greatness. Every dream you have ever thought, every person you've encountered, and every situation that was presented was not wasted. God uses all of it for our good and His Glory. *Parents, it's time to R.E.S.E.T.* is the guide that empowers you to push past limitations and lies in order to walk into your D.R.E.A.M (Divinely Revealed Event Awaiting Manifestation)."

–Naona Cole, Founder of
The Battlefield Babe, Veteran

"The smart, witty, and amazing Mr. Willie Tubbs really put his finger on the pulse of passionate and intelligent parenting in his phenomenally-on-point book *Parents, it's time to R.E.S.E.T.* I was enthralled, intrigued, and taken on a spiritual, emotional, and mental roller coaster ride in this life-healing and loving piece of literary excellence! In my honest opinion as a parent and an ordained minister of the Gospel, *Parents, it's time to R.E.S.E.T.* is truly a blessing to us all!"

–Chanti Amber Kelly, Evangelist,
Entrepreneur, Speaker, Author, and Coach

"*Parents, it's time to R.E.S.E.T.* is a great guide not only for parents but for anyone that needs to be empowered and pushed past limitations and fears. I was inspired and motivated to move past self-imposed barriers which got me stuck in one position. I would encourage others to read and take action on this book."

–Adele J. Foster-Glenn,
Author of *Do It First, Do It Right, Do It Better, Do It Now!*
The Road Map to Entrepreneurship

"Benjamin Franklin said it best: '… If you fail to plan, then plan to fail …' This book is a celebration, as well as blueprint, of one man's enthusiasm to overcome life-taught obstacles that he was predisposed to beyond his control. It teaches us to expect the unexpected and inspires us to search out our God-given reason for exlsting to find strength, happiness, and purpose. It was also a reminder that we must pass this greatness on, not only to inspire others but, most importantly, to become the type of role model that brings admiration from our own children that they may want to emulate. The whole book is permeated with love, fulfillment of expectations, and maintenance of important relationships. Absolutely a great read!"

–Stephenie Stewart, RN

"Wow, it's a must-read and have-your-tissues-ready. *Parents, it's time to R.E.S.E.T.* is one of the best books I have read. It changed my way of parenting. I had to observe myself on how I was raising my boys. I realized that I transported behaviors which I was taught into my parenthood. I had to quickly demolish those behaviors from my life. Being a parent is a learning and growing experience. This book has opened my eyes to be a better teacher, communicator, and listener. I cried on parts of the book because it was relatable to my childhood. If you don't have a copy, go and get yours now. It will be a game changer in your life. Thank you, Willie, for writing this book; it has truly encouraged me, and it will for others as well. I'm ready for the next book."

–Wendy Morgan, Teacher

"With great joy, my wife and I purchased and read Mr. Willie Tubbs's new book. All I can say is wow!!! It's powerful, practical, and full of wisdom tips! I have watched him continually grow into the powerhouse that he has become. He is an incredible family man who has served our country in the Armed Forces. He now serves his family with humility and excellence, and he has served up a book that every parent ought to read! He walks his talk and is an example of what he teaches. So, this book will keep you from being a mediocre parent, or being a mediocre parent will keep you from this book!

–Dr. Stan Harris, aka Dr. BreakThrough
Minister, Martial Artist,
Master Motivator, Marketer, and Mentor
www.DrBreakThrough.com

TABLE OF CONTENTS

Dedication

This book is dedicated to my Heavenly Father. Thank You for allowing me to share my testimony.

To my daughters, Ashanti and Vatanie; thank you for believing in me. Let this book demonstrate that you can do all things through Christ who strengthens you.

To my wife, Ladonna; thank you for helping me to be the best father that I can be.

To my mother, Dorothy; thank you for teaching me about life.

To my two brothers and sister, Anthony, Jerry, and Cloritha; thank you for being there whenever I needed you the most.

To all my nieces, Shaniqua, Deyshia, Desiray, Amani, and Jai; my nephews, Raiquan, Tyrese, and Jerry Jr.; I love you and thank you for being an inspiration in my life.

To my grandparents, Lou Willie Monroe and Emmitt Monroe; I know you are checking on me every day from Heaven. Thank you for everything you have done in my life.

To Aunt Carolyn, Aunt Merilyn, Uncle Jack, Aunt Sandra, Aunt Connie, Aunt Birda, Uncle Lonnie, Uncle Emmitt Jr., Laquita Gaines, Latoya Gaines, Latonya Gaines, Stephanie Coleman Steward, Jacqueline Wallace, Candace Monroe, Crystal Monroe, Larry Smith, Carmen Monroe, Carra Monroe, and to all the other family members I didn't mention; thank you all for being my family members.

To the late Myles Munroe; thank you for teaching me the difference between religion and the Kingdom of God.

To Dr. Stan Harris (aka Dr. Breakthrough), my business partner, speaking mentor and friend; thank you for showing me the way!

Finally, to all the parents out there who want to inspire their children to reach their greatness; I pray this book will educate and encourage you to become world-class parents.

Preface

REASON 1- MY FAMILY

Steve Harvey's friend was seeing his dying grandmother for the last time in the hospital. He invited Steve to go along with him for support.

When they arrived in the room, he (Steve's friend) kept saying to his grandmother, "I love you, I love you, I love you." His grandmother said, "Baby, I'm not going to make it; I'm going home. I called you to my room to ask you a question: Do you know your great-grandfather's name?" He said, "No." She then said, "You don't know his name because he didn't leave you anything. When I die, I want you to leave this place and live your life to the fullest, so your children's grandchildren will know your name. And the only way they will know who you are is that you have to leave them with something."

When I first heard this story, chills rolled down my back. I said to myself that I was going to live a life that my descendants will know my name.

One way my descendants will know my name is writing this book. I realize that writing a book makes a person IMMORTAL. Books will still exist when you are dead and gone. Even God knows the importance of writing a book because He wrote one Himself—the Bible.

I want to inspire you to write a book to leave a legacy for your children's grandchildren and to break the curse of fear and incompetence.

REASON 2- THE OPPORTUNITY TO CHANGE LIVES

My daughter Ashanti came home from school one day and said to me, "Dad, my friend Jasmine is not eating at school."

"Why is she not eating her lunch?" I asked.

"I don't know," Ashanti replied.

"Find out tomorrow and let me know," I said.

"OK," she said.

The next day, when Ashanti returned from school, she said to me, "I found out that she doesn't have any money for lunch."

"OK, I'm going to pay for her lunch for the remainder of the school year," I said. I also found out that the cafeteria was going to offer her a cheese sandwich because she didn't have money for a regular lunch. This is called 'lunch shaming.' We as a nation are having this issue in our schools. Lunch shaming is the term that defines a scenario where the cafeteria worker is ordered by the school to throw a child's lunch into the trash or offer a cheese sandwich in front of the child's peers.

Nelson Mandela made a profound statement when he said: "There can be no keener revelation of a society's soul than the way in which it treats its children."

Recently, some states passed a bill to stop this nonsense. But now, the schools are accumulating debt arising from unpaid lunch dues. I feel sad seeing that people who are incarcerated receive free food and education while the future leaders of this nation have to worry about being shamed, having low self-esteem, and having to face bullying.

Our government can only do so much to help, and I have decided to take matters into my own hand. Why? Because I personally know how it feels to have no money for lunch, and I don't want this to happen to any child anymore. So, I asked God, "What can I do to solve this problem?" God told me to write out the following four points and follow His lead:

1. Anointed Generals

Anointed Generals are leaders who have decided to rescue themselves, lead all children to their greatness, and help other leaders to learn the R.E.S.E.T. philosophy. As you can see, this book is designed to do just that.

2. Eradicate Negligence

There are so many people hurting emotionally in this world. Most people wouldn't reveal to their friends when they're hurting because of trust and shame. I then asked myself: *How can I minister help to people without even speaking to them, and how can I encourage people to approach me to help them with their problems?*

Well, I came up with an idea to solve the problem for our children, the schools, and the people who are hurting emotionally—all at the same time.

3. Through Serving Our Fellow Community Hang-ups

The number one approach to solving any problem in any community is to have unity. Even God said that nothing will restrain a community from their vision when they come together. Genesis 11:6 says, "And the LORD said, Behold, the people is one, and they have all one language; and this they begin to do: and now nothing will be restrained from them, which they have imagined to do."

To exemplify unity in the community, we started an apparel company. Every month, on a certain day, the members of the community will wear a T-shirt that will minister to people. Each T-shirt purchase will pay for a child's breakfast and lunch.

The T-shirts are not just regular T-shirts; they are designed to **SPARK ATTENTION** and give **INSTANT INSPIRATION**.

4. And Nurturing Growth Empowerment

My brothers and sisters, it's time to hire yourself and become a Kingdom-preneur. A Kingdom-preneur is one who is empowered by God to provide a product or service to people for profit with pleasure to promote the **Kingdom** while honoring the **King of Kings**.

You can be a Kingdom-preneur by becoming a paid walking billboard for God, and all you have to do is three things:

- 1st thing is, don't change. Continue recommending and promoting things just like you always have done—like your favorite restaurants and movies.
- 2nd thing is, join this movement
- 3rd thing is, help us spread the word by sharing this movement to one person a month. Within a year, this could be your full-time gig.

If you look at the first letter in each word that makes up the four points, you will notice it spells out a word. **A**nointed **G**enerals **E**radicate **N**egligence **T**hrough **S**erving **O**ur **F**ellow **C**ommunity **H**ang-ups **A**nd **N**urturing **G**rowth **E**mpowerment.

A.G.E.N.T.S. O.F. C.H.A.N.G.E. LLC

This is the name of the company. No gimmicks or gotchas. Go to the web address below to find out more details about this amazing opportunity. Remember that people are P.O.O.R. because they Pass Over Opportunities Repeatedly. Don't let this opportunity pass you by.

www.agentsofchangellc.com

Introduction

"First Sergeant Torres, I want to become an NCO (Non-Commissioned Officer)."

"Great, Specialist Tubbs!" he said with excitement. "OK, Specialist Tubbs, if you want to, an NCO must know the difference between an E-5, Sergeant, and NCO. Do you know the difference?" he asked.

I thought to myself if this was a trick question because it's all the same—or so I thought. I went ahead to answer him by saying, "There isn't a difference between the three, First Sergeant Torres."

"There is a difference. Let me explain it to you, and don't ever forget this:

- An E-5 is a pay grade. Some people are in a leadership position because of the money.

- A Sergeant is a rank. Some people are in a leadership position because of the authority it gives them.

- An NCO (Non-Commissioned Officer) is a leader. Some people are in a leadership position because they LEAD BY EXAMPLE."

First Sergeant Torres went on to say, "If you want this leadership position because of the money, people will HATE you! If you want a leadership position because of the authority the position gives, people will HATE you. If you want a leadership position because you want to influence people to reach their greatness, people will LOVE you!"

Please understand this, parents:

1. You can't lead your children into their greatness if you don't care about their future.

2. You can't point your children toward their greatness by using the dictatorship method.

3. You CAN lead your children into their greatness by demonstrating how you are reaching your greatness!

As parents...

- We want our children to follow God.

- We want our children to have a positive mentality.

- We want our children to bounce back from adversity.

- We want our children to have the confidence to achieve anything they want in life.

If you want any of these things for your children, you must LEAD BY EXAMPLE.

In this book, you will discover how to LEAD BY EXAMPLE. In fact, my RESET philosophy will show you how to:

1. Rescue yourself.

2. Lead your children to their greatness.

3. Pursue a career that will give you an opportunity to experience a level of fulfillment and happiness.

Are you willing to get out of your own way to become unstoppable in achieving every parenting goal you set for yourself?

This book, *Parents, it's time to R.E.S.E.T.*, has been designed to RESET your mind to believe you can rescue yourself and lead your children to their greatness:

- Regardless if the odds are all stacked against you.

- Regardless if you are parenting alone.

- Regardless if you feel you have already failed as a parent.

As a lifetime student of influence and mastering the art of leadership, I have read and tested hundreds of the best books and articles about parenting. This book is for the parents who desire to inspire their child(ren) to become everything God has destined them to be. You can achieve this through the implementation of the principles contained in this helpful how-to guide.

To rescue yourself and lead your children to their greatness, you must focus on wearing five different hats.

1. Purposed role model- a parent who inspires their children to reach their purpose by demonstrating how they are reaching their own.

2. Priestly role model- a parent who inspires their children to follow Christ by demonstrating how Christ has changed their own lives.

3. Positive role model- a parent who inspires their children to have a positive mentality by demonstrating how a positive mentality is affecting them.

4. Practical role model- a parent who inspires their children to overcome adversity by demonstrating how they overcame adversity.

5. Performance role model- a parent who inspires their children to celebrate their achievements by demonstrating how they celebrate theirs.

Anthony Monroe, a parent and inventor from North Dakota, has this to say: "There is a principle in this book that helps me solve problems, not just in parenting but in all other areas of my life."

I promise that if you apply the principles in this book, your child will not just be inspired by you but will also appreciate and admire you.

Don't be the person who misses out on opportunities. Be the kind of person that people marvel at. Be the type of person that takes massive action.

This book will not disappoint you; the principles weren't just proven in my life but also the lives of many people in the Bible. Take control of your life now and enjoy the new life you are creating.

CHAPTER ONE

If Your Why Doesn't Make You Cry, then You Must Find Another Why

Strength is when you have so much to cry for, but you prefer to smile instead.
–Author Unknown

The Miracle Child

Son: "Mama, I'm home."

Mom: "How was school, son?"

Son: "It was OK."

Mom: "Did you learn anything new today?"

Son: "No, Ma'am."

Mom: "Are you OK, son?"

Son: "To be honest, Mama, my feelings are hurt."

Mom: "Why are your feelings hurt?"

Son: "Well, today at school, I was looking for a   particular book to read. I knew it was going to be hard to read, but I decided that I was going to give it a try. When I picked the book up, my teacher said the book is too advanced for me, and I should look for a less developed book. I dropped my head and said, 'OK.'"

Mom: "She said THAT? Sweetie, come and sit down next to me. Son, have I ever told you about you being a miracle baby?"

Son: "What do you mean miracle baby?"

Mom: "OK, son, let me explain. Before you, I had already given birth to Anthony, Clorithia, and Jerry. While in labor with Jerry, I had so much pain that I told the doctor to tie, cut, and burn my tubes so I wouldn't have any more children. Well, three years later, I became pregnant with you. I cried and said to myself, 'I don't want this baby. The doctors made a mistake.' I went to your grandfather and said, 'Daddy, I can't have this baby. The pain from the last delivery was too unbearable, and I can't afford another child. I refuse to have this baby. I want to have an abortion.'

Your grandfather said, 'OK, Dorothy, here is the money for the abortion.'

"When the conversation ended, your granny started crying in the kitchen. Your grandfather walked in the kitchen and asked, 'Lou, what is wrong?' Mama Lou said, 'Y'all are murderers! Y'all are trying to kill my grandbaby.' Then Daddy Emmitt said, 'I'm not a G&@d*&# murderer!' He then walked back to me and said, 'Give me my money back, Dorothy. I'm not a G&@d*&# murderer!' So, I didn't have a choice but to give the money back. Eight months later, I had you. And when I saw your face for the first time, I said, 'Thank You, God, for this angel. He is not a mistake; he is a miracle!'"

(Tears started running down the child's face.)

Son: "Do you think that if Daddy Emmitt wouldn't have taken his money back from you, I wouldn't be here today?"

Mom: "If it weren't for your granny crying, I would have to say no." She hugged him and said, "I love you, and never forget that. Remember, you can do anything you want in life."

The boy in the story is me, and I was eight years old when my mother told me that story. Now I'm 35, I still tear up and laugh whenever I share that story. The moral of the story is that my grandmother's WHY made her CRY. This

MOTIVATED my grandfather to take RESPONSIBILITY and do the right thing. It's funny how you learn a life principle and realize your life story was based on that principle. From that moment on, I knew God had a unique plan for me to accomplish on this earth.

> *All that I am, or hope to be, I owe to my angel mother.*
> –Abraham Lincoln

Do you have a WHY that will make you CRY, that will ignite a MOVEMENT in you to do the things you should have started a long time ago? While studying the life of Jesus Christ, I realized that His WHY made him cry when He was pursuing His dream to save God's people from being lost. It was recorded that He wept three times publicly: He wept over Lazarus (John 11:35). He cried for Jerusalem (Luke 13:34). He wept while on the cross (Hebrews 5:7).

While on the cross, the writer Matthew said that there was darkness from the sixth hour to the ninth hour before Jesus cried out, "My God, my God, why hast thou forsaken me?" (Matthew 27:45–46). This is very profound to me because this darkness is not just the usual darkness, like when the sun goes down or when the storm hovers over the land. This darkness has a purpose. This darkness represents God's defining moment for change. Your defining moment for change is here as well.

I couldn't imagine living in a state that didn't reach the ocean. It was a giant reset button. You could go to the edge of the land and see infinity and feel renewed.
–Avery Sawyer

Responsibility

A couple of years ago, I was listening to Tony Robbins while driving my car. He mentioned something that was very profound. He said, "Two things motivate humans: pain and pleasure." I thought to myself, *if a person is in a lot of pain, they will make an instant decision to get out of their misery. But if their pleasure overrides their pain, they will find themselves going back to the pain.*

Let me explain: Do you know anyone that suffers from gout? Gout is a form of arthritis. I have a friend that suffers from this, and he isn't supposed to eat red meat. Every time he eats it, his knees swell up like bowling balls. I asked him, "Why do you keep eating red meat?" He said, "Well, I can't help it. I love it."

Now, I want you to understand what God did in John 3:16. "For God so loved the world, that He gave His only begotten Son, that whosoever believeth in Him should not perish, but have everlasting life." Two things I want you to focus on are the word 'Loved' and the clause 'He gave His only begotten Son.'

Firstly, the Bible has several meanings of love, but this meaning of love is unconditional, agape love. This kind of love gave Jesus the power and reason to endure the pain before the cross and while He was on it. In other words, your CHILDREN will provide you with the ability and motivation to take any pain.

The Bible says in 1 John 4:18, "There is no fear in love. But perfect love drives out fear." When I first read that Scripture, I didn't understand it until a friend, John Perez from Quanah, Texas, illustrated it to me.

"Can you swim?" he asked.

"Yes, I can swim," I replied.

"Let's say you can't swim. Now picture your daughter jumping in the lake, and she starts drowning. Will you jump in the lake to save her?" he asked.

"Of course, I will!" I replied.

"OK, that's perfect love," he said. "You bypass your fear because of the love that you have for your child."

Secondly, God loved His people so much that He gave His Son the mission to save His people. Jesus is also God Himself, aka the Trinity (John 8:58). In other words, God took the responsibility upon Himself to save His own people. In fact, He even promised satan that He would send His Son to crush his head (in Genesis 3:15) and pay the debt in full.

As a parent, you must take full responsibility for your life! You must take full responsibility for your relationship with God and your children. You must take full responsibility for your finances. You must take full responsibility for your health. To put everything in perspective, feeling pain from your perfect love will make you responsible for doing the right thing.

A Friend's Cry for Help

Me: "Hello, this is Willie Tubbs."

Tony: "Hey, Sgt. Tubbs! This is Tony!"

Me: "Tony, my battle buddy from the military?"

Tony: "Yes, sir! It is me, Willie."

Me: "It's been a long time—over ten years, I think. How are you?"

Tony: "Well, Sgt. Tubbs, I'm calling you because I figured if I can't talk to anybody, I know I can tell you."

Me: "Yes, sir, I'm always here for my battle. What's on your mind?"

Tony: "My girl and I are having a lot of troubles lately, and I think we are on the verge of breaking up. I care about her so much. I'm willing to work it out, but it seems that she wants to go back to the same lifestyle that she was running from when I first met her."

Me: "Is she willing to work it out?"

Tony: "I don't think so. She is giving me the runaround. She said she does, but her actions say she doesn't. Don't think of me differently, battle, but sometimes, I feel like killing myself!"

Me: "WAIT! WAIT! WAIT! First of all, battle (military term for buddy), please don't ever forget that YOU MATTER! Even though I haven't seen you or talked to you in ten years, I would be willing to fly anywhere in the world to be your support system. Secondly, you have a daughter that needs you. How would your daughter feel if you ended your life for a woman that doesn't want you? Thirdly, I don't think differently of you because, sometimes, life gets hard. But remember, suicide is a permanent solution to a temporary problem."

Tony: "You are right, battle. My daughter does need me, and I knew I could talk to you. I called you because I was on my last leg."

Me: "Do you want me to come see you?"

Tony: "No, battle, I'm okay now. I'm going to focus on my daughter from here on out."

Me: "Bro, let me pray for you. Heavenly Father......In Jesus' name. Amen!"

Tony: "Thank you, Sgt. Tubbs. Bye."
Me: "Bye."

When the call was over, I thanked God for allowing me to be available to help my friend. He said I was his only option left. I thanked God for giving him the inclination that he matters to the world and to his daughter. I truly believe that if I didn't have him feel his daughter's pain, then he would have gone through the process to kill himself.

*UPDATE: Tony called me on this past Father's Day 2018 and said life is excellent now. He moved to a different location and found a new job.

*The **aim of the wise is not to secure pleasure, but to avoid pain.***
–Aristotle

I Need a Deck of Cards

Ray Lewis: "Mama, will you buy me a deck of cards?"

His mother: "Junior, I don't allow gambling in this house."

Ray Lewis: "Mama, I don't need it for gambling. I just need a deck of cards."

Ray Lewis said that his mama took so much physical abuse for years, and he couldn't help her because he wasn't strong enough. He didn't have the muscle, and every time a man hit her, she would bleed from her eyes. She would wear sunglass in the house.

After the last altercation with his stepfather, Ray ran into the garage with his deck of cards. He flipped a 7 and did seven pushups. He flipped a 6 and did six pushups. He flipped a 9 and did nine pushups. He flipped a 2 and did two pushups. He continued until he got all the way through the deck. He then flipped the deck and started the sit-ups. He wanted to make sure that sports wasn't the reason why he couldn't train. His reason was to make sure nobody put their hands on his mother again.

Ray Lewis is known as the best linebacker ever in the history of football. He was a First Ballot Hall of Famer. He played for the Baltimore Ravens for 17 years. They erected a statue of him in front of the stadium. All through his accomplishments, it was his mother that gave him his WHY which made him take responsibility for becoming great in his football career.

The Budgeting Machine

My wife, Ladonna, is a budgeting machine. I remember one day she was on her bank's website. She realized her account was missing a penny. She became furious and called the bank to discuss her bank account. I looked at her and said, "It's a penny, sweetie." Then she said, "I don't care."

I asked Ladonna where she got her passion for budgeting. She said, "When I was young, my mom and dad made good money, but at times, our lights were turned off. There were times when they placed clothing over our blankets to keep us warm at night. That feeling was a horrible feeling, and I promised myself that my children would never suffer as I did."

We have been married for over 15 years, and not a day goes by that she doesn't check her bank book. In essence, she felt the pain her children would face in the future if she didn't budget. This motivated her to be responsible.

My children are the reason I laugh, smile and want to get up every morning.
–Gena Lee Nolin

The Fatherless Child

Growing up, I didn't have my father present in my life. I still can remember when I was in second grade. The school wanted to honor parents by inviting them to eat with their child(ren) in the cafeteria.

The school placed the students with their parents in the CENTER of the cafeteria, and the students without their parents ate by themselves on the side of the cafeteria.

There were about seven or eight students sitting by themselves, eating, and about 40 students sitting with their parents. I can remember saying to myself, *I wish my parents were here.* My mom was a single mom raising four kids by herself. She worked all the time to provide for the family, as my father wasn't around to help her. As I contemplated more and more about my situation, I started to feel alone and abandoned. My eyes welled up with tears, which started flowing down my face. I said to myself, *I will never allow this to happen to my kids.*

I went on to junior high school and still didn't have any support, and there was no sign of my father around. I went on to high school and competed in track and field. I remember my coach always wanted me to run the anchor leg in the sprint relay. Marques Turner, a friend of mine, ran the third leg. We won first place most of the time.

One school day, my friend Marques said, "Willie, do you know a man named Floyd Turner?" I told him, "I heard that he's supposed to be my dad." Then he looked at me and said, "He is my dad too." I was in shock! My friend was my half-brother. Crazy, huh?

A couple of days later, I met my dad while working at Taco Bell. He came to me and asked, "Are you Willie Tubbs?" I said, "Yes." He then said, "I'm Floyd Turner." My whole world stopped! I took a break from work, and we both sat down to talk. It was a great conversation, and I felt fulfilled, but two years later, he died of cancer!

My childhood wasn't comfortable, but it was necessary! God knew I had to be raised a certain way to bring the BEAST out of me, so I would be able to break the curse in my family and the world.

I want you to read some stats on what happens if a father isn't PRESENT in their children's lives. I found this information on www.fatherhood.com:

1. In America, 23.6% of children lived in father-absent homes in 2014. Consequently, there is a "father factor" in nearly all of the societal issues facing America today.

2. Children living in female-headed homes with no spouse present have a poverty rate of 47.6%—over four times the rate of children living in married couple families.

3. Father involvement in schools is associated with the higher likelihood of a student getting mostly A's. This was true for fathers in biological parent families, for stepfathers, and for fathers heading single-parent families. Additionally, students living in father-absent homes are twice as likely to repeat a grade in school.

4. Children born to single mothers show higher levels of aggressive behavior than children born to married mothers. Living in a single-mother household is equivalent to experiencing 5.25 partnership transitions.

5. A study of 109 juvenile offenders indicated that family structure significantly predicts delinquency.

6. 92% of parents in prison are fathers, and between 1991 and 2007, the number of children with an incarcerated father grew 79%.

7. The National Longitudinal Survey of Youth found that obese children are more likely to live in father-absent homes than are non-obese children.

8. Researchers using a pool from both the U.S. and New Zealand found strong evidence that father absence has an effect on early sexual activity and teenage pregnancy. Teens without fathers were twice as likely to be involved in early sexual activity and seven times more likely to get pregnant as an adolescent.

9. 1 in 4 children live in a home without a dad.

10. Involved dads lead to less distress in toddler

I Understand

God revealed to me early in life why He allowed things to happen to us. He used a word that kindled my passion for acronyms. This word is LOVE. Now, let me break it down for you so you can understand:

The 'L' in the word LOVE means Longsuffering. We all must go through trials and tribulations in life. God will never allow you to be tempted beyond what you can bear. God knows you will triumph through your trial. 1 Corinthians 10:13 says, "Here hath no temptation taken you, but such as is common to man: but God is faithful, who will not suffer you to be tempted above that ye are able; but will with the temptation also make a way to escape, that ye may be able to bear it." Being a parent in this day and age is a very daunting but necessary task!

The 'O' in the word LOVE means Obedience. While we triumph through our trial, we must stay obedient to God. We can't curse God because we are going through the test. Some tests are short-lived, whereas others are long. Therefore, we must understand that STORM stands for Something That Only Remains Momentarily. We must push through it! Matthew 6:33 says, "But SEEK FIRST His kingdom and His righteousness, and all these things will be given to you as well." God's kingdom should be our center of focus.

The 'V' in the word LOVE means Victory. John 6:33 says, "I have said these things to you, that in Me you may have peace. In the world, you will have tribulation. But take heart; I have overcome the world." In essence, we have victory in Jesus! In fact, we become pearls in the world. Do you know how pearls are made? Pearls are made through the irritations of a clam. We become pearls through the irritations of life. When people see you like a pearl, when they look at this valuable piece of art, they will be drawn to you for your help.

The 'E' in the word LOVE means "Encourage someone else who is going through the same problem." I didn't have all the knowledge to become a world-class parent. But through the years, I researched, listened to other people, and experienced enough to provide content to help you. Luke 22:32 says, "But I have prayed for thee, that thy faith fails not: and when thou art converted, strengthen thy brethren."

We must help our brothers and sisters. It is our testimony that will transform the lives of other individuals. Revelation 12:11 says, "And they overcame him by the blood of the Lamb, and by the word of THEIR TESTIMONY, and they loved not their lives unto the death." Your children should be your WHY that makes you take responsibility for doing the right thing.

Principles

1. Your darkness has a purpose. Your darkness is your defining moment for change.

2. Two things motivate humans: pain and pleasure.

3. If a person is in a lot of pain, they will make an instant decision to get out of their misery. But if their pleasure overrides their pain, they will find themselves going back to the pain.

4. LOVE will always out power FEAR.

5. We become pearls through the irritations of life.

6. Your testimony is designed to strengthen you and your brethren.

Prayer

Father God, in the name of Jesus, we come to You because we need Your help. You said in Your Word that if we need anything, we can lift up our eyes onto the hills. From where comes our help? Our help comes from You, Father, who made Heaven and Earth. Father, show us our WHY that makes us cry, that will make us take responsibility for change. We thank You in advance in Jesus' name. Amen.

Questions

1. What is your WHY that makes you cry?

2. If you don't have children to care for, where else can you find your WHY?

3. What will happen to your WHY if you don't take charge of your life?

4. List some of your fears:

CHAPTER TWO

Remember, God Created You to Solve a Problem for Him

For he chose us in him before the creation of the world to be holy and blameless in his sight. In love.
–Ephesians 1:4

The Dream

Danny: "What are you working on, Willie?"

Me: "I'm working on my escape plan to leave this job."

Danny: "You just started here. Are you already trying to leave? This place is a good job. A person will never find another job making this kind of money in this area."

Me: "Yes, sir! This place is my third production job, and I can't see myself doing this all my life. My purpose is more than working for a living."

Danny: "Ha ha ha ha!"

Me: "What's so funny?"

Danny: "You're a LIFER!"

Me: "No, I'm 25 years old, and I have plans to change my world! I know people are laughing, but I will have the last laugh."

Danny: "I bet you 20 dollars that you will still be working here when I retire."

Me: "How many years do you have left to retire?"

Danny: "12 years."

Me: "OK. Deal! Danny, I see guys work for a company like this their entire lives. People exactly like you. They clock in and clock out places like this, and they never have a moment of happiness. I have an opportunity here."
Danny: "My opportunity will come when I retire."

Fast forward eight years. My co-worker Danny Stillwell died from a massive heart attack. He didn't have the opportunity to enjoy his retirement. I was one of his pallbearers at the funeral. After his death, I went to GOD and said, "What is my purpose? Why am I here? I don't want to do this for the rest of my life." God said, "Keep moving FORWARD (Focus On Real Wins And Remove Distractions)."

Everything changed when I discovered that God created me to solve a problem for Him.

It's time to R.E.S.E.T.

Sleep is our recharge function and our reset button ... and we all need a reset button sometimes.
–Sam Owen

In the Beginning ...

Genesis 1:1 says, "In the beginning ..." The word 'beginning' connotes time. Dictionary.com says that time is a system of events in the past, present, and future. We establish time regarding past and future events. We measure time in seconds, minutes, hours, days, months, and years. Also, we measure time through birth, growth, and death. But God experiences time differently than us. God lives in the eternal. In the eternal, time does not exist.

The question I asked myself and eventually God is this: "Why did God start my beginning?" I concluded that God started our beginning because He wanted us to exist along with Him in eternity—but in a different place called earth— to solve a problem for Him. Let me break it down so you can understand:

We all know that God is love, right? If God is love, He needs something to which He can express His love. Do you have a favorite sports team like the Dallas Cowboys and Golden State Warriors? Do you like athletic superstars like Usain Bolt, Michael Jordan, and LeBron James? You probably watch these teams or athletes play all the time. You might even buy a Dak Prescott, Ezekiel Elliott, Stephen Curry, Michael Jordan, or LeBron James jersey, right? But why? That very thing you love will consistently stay on your mind, and you will openly express how much it means to you.

Ephesians 1:4 says, "For He chose us in Him before the creation of the world to be holy and blameless in His sight." Also, Psalms 8: 4 says, "What is man, that thou art mindful of him? and the son of man, that thou visitest him?" These two Scriptures explain why God was thinking about us before the beginning, and He continues to think about us throughout our lives.

We are a spirit, we have a soul, and we live in a body. Do you agree? John 4:24 says, "God is a spirit, and His worshipers must worship in the Spirit and in truth." Owing to the fall of man, our body and soul will have to die. Romans 3:23 says, "For we all have sinned and fall short of the glory of God." Spirit never dies. These Scriptures explain why He wants us to exist alongside Him.

Then Paul says that we are ambassadors of Christ. 2 Corinthians 5:20 says, "We are, therefore, Christ's ambassadors, as though God were making His appeal through us. We implore you on Christ's behalf: Be reconciled with God." An ambassador is someone that's living in a country but represents a different country, right? This explains why God wanted us located in a different place called earth.

Now, I'm going to show you that we are here on earth to solve problems for God. Isaiah 46:9–10 (NIV) says, "Remember the former things, those of long ago; I am God, and there is no other; I am God, and there is none like me. I make known the end from the beginning, from ancient time, what is still to come. I say, 'My purpose will stand, and I will do all that I please.'"

I have to demonstrate this to you; I don't think you understood what you just read.

God says, "I finish first."

"Then I back up."

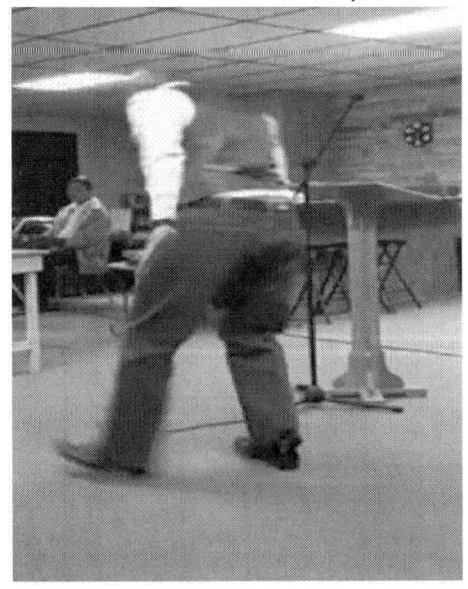

"And then I begin."

He said, "I make known the end from the beginning."
So, He finishes first!

Then He begins.

This is evidence that whatever God begins, it means it's already finished. Let me say it again: this is evidence that whatever God begins, it means it's already finished. And this also tells you that God will never begin anything unless it's finished first. Now, what did your father do? Your father sent sperm to your mother—over 600 million sperms—and God said, "I want that one!" Guess who that was? That was you!

God says, "I have finished something."

"Now, I'm going to start something."

Your birth is evidence that there's something that has been finished that you are supposed to start. I want that to sink in a little bit. Your birth is evidence that whatever is finished, you are supposed to start. Let me put it this way:

When God needed a Deliverer to go to Pharaoh and tell him to let His people go, He started Moses!

When God needed a Chief Economic Adviser to save the people in Egypt from starvation, He started Joseph!

When God needed a Savior to save His people from the pits of hell, He started Jesus!

When God needed a Financial and Business Teacher to help an average person to become an entrepreneur, He started Robert Kiyosaki, the author of *Rich Dad Poor Dad*.

When God needed a Relationship Educator to teach married couples how to fall in love with each other again, He started Dr. Gary Chapman, the author of *The 5 Love Languages*.

When God needed a National Leader to help minorities, especially the African-Americans, to believe that all things are possible, He started former President Barack Obama.

When God needed a Visionary Leader to explain our potential, the totality of the Kingdom of God, and leadership, He started Dr. Myles Munroe.

When God needed a man to become a FATHER FIGURE to thousands of orphans on the streets of Kenya, He started Charles Mully!

When God needed a Chief Breakthrough Officer to help people break through their strongholds by BREAKING INTO their desires, He started Dr. Stan Harris (aka Dr. Breakthrough).

When God needed a R.E.S.E.T. Coach to help people become world-class parents by showing them how to rescue themselves, lead your children to their greatness, and pursue a career that will give them an opportunity to experience a level of fulfillment and happiness, He started Willie Lee Tubbs.

Now, the question I want to ask you is: Why did God create you? What problem were you created to solve?

The biggest adventure you can take is to live the life of your dreams.
–Oprah Winfrey

Purposed Role Model

Our children are looking for a purposed role model to follow. A purposed role model is a parent who inspires their children to reach their purpose by demonstrating how they are reaching theirs.

Children don't need a parent who tells them they can do anything they want to do in life but sits back and plays it safe by going to a job they hate. Your children watch you come home every day complaining about your boss, co-workers, and how much more money you need. I used to do the same thing until I heard Jim Rohn say, "Don't wish your life was easier; wish that you were better." He also said, "Your life will change when you change." These sayings and many more affected my belief system. Therefore, I got M.A.D. at my situation, and I **Made A Decision** to change my life.

When I saw my children the next time, I told them that it's OK to have heroes and sheroes in life, but I'm going to be their number one role model. They will see firsthand how a person can start from the bottom and make it all the way to the top.

Paul said in 1 Corinthians 11:1, "Be ye followers of me, even as I also am of Christ." I started working on myself and realized the need to pursue my own happiness.

You Must Pursue Your Own Happiness!

The acronym JOB stands for people who Jump Out of the Bed to go on the Journey Of Boredom to work a job to be Just Over Broke.

Did you know that most employers pay their employees just enough so they won't quit? Did you know that most employees work just enough so they won't get fired? In the meantime, both parties are settling. God never meant for anyone to settle in anything in their life. There is something inside you that must come out of you to serve the world, and it is called your gift.

The Bible says in Proverbs 18:16, "Your gift will make room for you and bring you before great men." Les Brown said, "We weren't meant to work for a living but to live our making, and living our making will make our living."

WAIT A MINUTE! GO BACK AND READ THAT AGAIN!

When I first heard that, I ran out of my house. This quote states that we need to stop chasing money and start pursuing purpose.

I also heard Les Brown tell a story about George Bernard Shaw that resonated with me. Toward the end of

Mr. Shaw's life, someone asked him: "If you had to be anybody throughout history, and if you had the power to be born again, who would you like to be?" George Bernard Shaw said without hesitation, "I would like to be the man I never was." In essence, he was dying with his music still in him. In other words, he believed he had potential that was always hidden within, but he was too afraid to bring it out.

Every time I hear the above-mentioned story, I think of Jesus Christ saying on the cross, "It is finished" (John 19:30). We humans think longevity is the goal of life, but nothing could be further from the truth. Methuselah was the oldest person in the Bible. The only thing the Bible says about this person is that he had children and died at the age of 969. I'm not saying there's something wrong with living a long life; the question is, are you effective while you are living a long life?

When Martin Luther King Jr. realized his purpose was to lead the civil rights movement, he wasn't concerned about the longevity of life. Read this excerpt from his famous speech *I've Been to the Mountaintop*:

> But it really doesn't matter with me now, because I've been to the mountaintop. And I don't mind. Like anybody, I would like to live a long life. Longevity has its place. But I'm not concerned about that now. I just want to do God's will. And He's allowed me to go up to the mountain. And I've

looked over. And I've seen the Promised Land. I may not get there with you. But I want you to know tonight that we, as a people, will get to the Promised Land!"

When I think of people that impacted the world but lived a short life, a couple of names pop up, like Jesus Christ who died at the age of 33, Martin Luther King Jr. who died at the age of 39, Malcolm X who died at the age of 39, Bruce Lee who died at the of 32, John Lennon who died at the age of 40, etc.

When I think of the individuals who lived long and still had an impact, names pop up too—people like Nelson Mandela, Mother Teresa, Rosa Parks, Mahatma Gandhi, Helen Keller, Myles Munroe, and the list goes on and on. It's not the quantity of life everyone should strive for; it's the quality of life we all should pursue.

The Power of Influence

The most important influence in my childhood was my father.
–DeForest Kelley

I was in 3rd grade in Wichita Falls, TX. My brother Jerry came home every day talking about a particular 7th-grade teacher named Mr. Blow. I never saw my brother so excited about history. Every day, after school, I couldn't wait to get home to hear Jerry talk about Mr. Blow. I used to get so excited myself that I also couldn't wait to get to 7th grade. I wanted to have him as my history teacher.

You can tell if a person is appointed or anointed for a career. Mr. Blow was anointed to be a 7th-grade History teacher. Most teachers these days are there for a paycheck. So, my question for you is, are you just working for a paycheck?

You can influence your children by just pursuing your dream. My mother did this very thing, not knowing it would leave an impression on her children's life. Let me explain:

I was in 7th grade, living in Giddings, Texas. My mother started a Janitorial Cleaning business called DH (Dorothy Hicks) Services. She had two major cleaning contracts she was handling in LaGrange and Pflugerville respectively, both in Texas. The contract in LaGrange was to clean a power plant every weekend. The one in Pflugerville was to clean a movie theater every night.

Watching my mother work her business helped me understand the ins and outs of it. I didn't really understand how 'BIG' she was doing it until my friend's mother knocked on my door, looking for my mother for a job. I said to myself, *My mother is DOING IT BIG.*

I can still remember my mother working so hard that she was burnt out in six months. She had one day off in the six-month stretch. She made good money, about $42,000 in her first four months. But since she didn't educate herself on how to maintain the business, she gave her business up and got a regular job.

I applaud her so much for taking a chance on herself. Most people would have played it safe. She made so big an impression on her children that my brother Jerry started and maintained his own trucking company. I started and managed three online businesses. Anthony, my oldest brother, is an inventor. Cloritha, my sister, is a customer service expert. Once again, I would like to thank my mother.

I remember when I was learning how to make an app for my online business. My business partners (Melvin, Anthony, Corrie, and Meke) and I had come together to start a company called Your Passion Line. I posted our company's app on Google Play Store. Well, one day, my daughter said with excitement, "Daddy, today we had an assignment to do in class, and we were asked to take out our phones to search for a particular app. While on Google Play Store, I wondered if your app was on the store. I looked up Your Passion Line and saw your photo next to it. I got up and showed all my friends and said, 'My daddy made his own app.'"

I then asked her if she was proud of her dad, and she replied, "Yes, I am!"

When she told me that, I thought to myself, *when parents do something significant in their child's eyes, they will admire them and won't be shy to tell their peers about it.*

Multiple Streams of Income

Success is really about your mindset.
–F. Gary Gray

A couple of months ago, I was talking to a friend about his dream. Tyler's dream is to be a police officer, but he told me the pay isn't enough for him to pursue it. I said to him that he would never be happy until he becomes a policeman. I also told him that there are many ways to make money on the side so that he can focus on his passion.

Tyler replied, "My father told me that the only way to make money is through hard work."

I said, "Correct, but it's half the truth. Hard work is on one side of the coin, but leverage is on the other." I then began to speak to him about something he had never heard before: "Tyler, we were taught to trade hours for dollars and work hard with our hands. The problem is, we only have two hands. What will happen if you become sick or if the company decides to do massive layoff? What will happen if you need to take care of a family member? Most people will offer prayers when you are in need of a financial blessing, which is good, but when are we going to be at a point in our life where we become the financial blessing that people need?"

January 11, 2017, Solvay in Vernon, Texas, laid off over half of their workforce. And yes, I was one of those people that were laid off. And boy let me tell you, it was a SAD day. It wasn't sad for me because I had done something two years prior to set my family up for financial success.

When they called out the names of those being laid off, I saw a dark cloud hover over the whole plant. I was the only one that was smiling the entire day. A couple of people went on Facebook to vent. After seeing ten posts, I decided to do a video to inspire and educate everyone on the importance of having multiple streams of income. The theme of the video was based on Ecclesiastes 11:

> [1] Ship your grain across the sea; after many days, you may receive a return. [2] Invest in seven ventures, yes, in eight; you do not know what disaster may come upon the land ...

> [6] Sow your seed in the morning, and at evening, let your hands not be idle, for you do not know which

will succeed, whether this or that, or whether both will do equally well.

"Sow your seed in the morning ..." What does that mean? It means that you should work hard for the company that employed you. In the evening, when you arrive home, WORK on something that will provide an extra stream of income. In the end, you may not know which one will succeed. Now, if you have seven or eight streams of income, you will have an opportunity to do what you love instead of doing what you have to do.

Let me put it this way: Everyone can't be a CEO (Chief Executive Officer). Everyone can't be a COO (Chief Operating Officer). But EVERYBODY can be a CLO (Chief Leveraging Officer).

Archimedes said it the best when he said, "If I had a lever long enough and prop strong enough, I could single-handedly move the world."

Jesus Christ is the master of leveraging things to perform miracles: Jesus leveraged a boy's lunch to feed over five thousand (John 6:9). Jesus leveraged mud to heal a blind man (John 9:6). Jesus leveraged a fish to pay His taxes (Matthew 17:27).

Now read this quote from Warren Buffet: "If you don't find a way to make money while in your sleep, you will work until you die." You must find a way to make money while in your sleep to buy back your time. You spend money while you sleep. Therefore, you must make money while you sleep. How do we spend money 24 hours of the day? While you sleep, how many times does the A/C unit, refrigerator, or deep freezer turn off and on? Think about it ...

Understand this, if you want to find a way to make money while you sleep, you must switch your thinking from the WAGE system into the PROFIT SYSTEMS (Save Your Self Time, Energy, Money, and Stress).

In 2019, this book will have been released. Here's how I plan to repurpose the contents to create multiple streams of income:

1. The physical book will be one stream of income.

2. I'm also turning the book into an audiobook. That's another stream of income.

3. I'm also turning the book into an online course. That's another stream of income.

4. I'm also turning the book into a webinar. That's another stream of income.

5. I'm also turning the book into an e-book. That's another stream of income.

6. I'm also turning the book into a live event. That's another stream of income.

OK, from that one idea, I can repurpose the contents into six different streams of income. You can do the same thing. Everybody has a story to tell that will BLESS everyone.

Leave a Legacy

A good man leaveth an inheritance to his children's children:
and the wealth of the sinner is laid up for the just.
–Proverbs 13:22

The acronym DREAM stands for Divinely Revealed Event Awaiting Manifestation. Your dream is waiting on you. You must understand that your life is personal but not private. Your life is not just yours, and you can't do whatever you want.

We all have an area of influence (aka our children) that's always looking at us and unconsciously following our actions. That's why if the parents are unstable most likely the children will grow up to be unstable too.

Check this out: Your dream is like a seed. When you start pursuing your dream, you begin to water that seed, which evidently grows up into a tree that produces fruit.

But guess what?

The fruit that's on a tree is never there for its own enjoyment; it's for other people to enjoy. Your fruit is your legacy. Your life is not just yours. Please pursue that dream so your family, friends, and the world can eat your fruit. This book is my fruit, and I'm sharing it with you to help you enjoy your life in parenting. What kind of life do you want to leave for your children and the world?

Financial freedom should be one of your goals! Some people may say, "Money is the root of all evil." But when you quote 1 Timothy 6:10, make sure you quote the whole Scripture. It says, "For the love of money is the root of all evil: which while some coveted after, they have erred from the faith, and pierced themselves through with many sorrows." You must love it for it to be evil!

We should look for ways to make money for others who can't make money for themselves. I like what Psalm 23 says: "thou anointest my head with oil; my cup runneth over." When I read that, I thought, *if my cup is running over, then the table has an opportunity to receive the anointing.*

Now the anointing doesn't stop at the table if the cup continues to run over. It will fall on the ground so that everything will be affected by the anointing. Now picture this anointing is in the form of money.

My mentor Dr. Stan explained what money really is. He said, "Money is nothing but a way of keeping score on how much value you give to the world." STOP! DID YOU GET THAT? That's worth saying again. "Money is nothing but a way of keeping score on how much value you give to the world." If you don't have any money, ask yourself how much value you are serving to the world.

You need multiple streams of money to help your children to pursue their dreams. One of the worst feelings in the world is to be a parent who has a child that knows his or her purpose, the child is looking for you to help him or her, and you don't have the funds to help.

Having multiple streams of income allows us the opportunity to give our children more ATTENTION. The first thing our children crave is our ATTENTION. They want us to be available for the sporting events. They want us to be available for parent-teacher conferences. They want us to support them in everything. Money can't buy you happiness, but it will give you more options.

A Purposed Role Model is a parent who inspires their children to reach their purpose by demonstrating how they are reaching theirs. To do this, you must pursue your own happiness, seek multiple streams of income, pursue to leave a legacy, and seek to give your children the attention they need.

There are only two lasting bequests we can hope to give our children. One of these is roots, the other, wings.
–Johann Wolfgang von Goethe

Principles

1. God will never begin anything unless it's finished first.

2. Everyone on earth is a problem solver.

3. Children love to see their parents succeed in their purpose.

4. Everyone is waiting on you to eat your fruit.

5. Your purpose will provide happiness.

6. Achieving financial independence will redeem the time for you and your children.

7. Having multiple streams of income motivates you to take more risks.

8. Life isn't about longevity; it's about being effective while you are living.

Prayer

Father God, in the name of Jesus, thank You for this moment. Father, some people may not know their meaning for living. But we decree and declare right now that they will find their purpose. We also pray for financial freedom for everyone who seeks more time to be with their children. In Jesus' name. Amen.

Questions

1. Do you know your purpose for living?

2. What are your passions?

3. What can you do all day long without receiving pay?

4. What comes naturally to you but hard for others?

5. What do other people say when you do well?

6. Do you believe it's wrong to pursue Financial Freedom?

7. How will your children feel if money isn't an issue for them to pursue their dream?

CHAPTER THREE

Embrace Your Mentor's Mentality

A mentor is someone who sees more talent and ability within you, than you see in yourself, and helps bring it out of you.
–Bob Proctor

The Awakening

It was 4 p.m. August 29, 2000. I was a senior in high school. I walked into my house after school was out for that day, and the conversation went thus:

Me: "Hey, Jennifer, what are you doing here?"

Jennifer (my girlfriend): "I came here to surprise you. How was school?"

Me: "School was the same. You know how it is. Do you miss it?"

Jennifer: "I miss my friends and some teachers. I'm glad I graduated last year."

Me: "Where are my mother and Marvin?"

Jennifer: "Well, Willie, sit down and let me tell you."

Me: "Is anything wrong?"

Jennifer: "OK, I came here to surprise you, and your mother said that she and Marvin are moving to Electra. She wanted me to tell you."

Me: "WHAT! They moved to Electra! When did they leave?"

Jennifer: "They left three hours ago."

Me: "They couldn't even stop by the school to tell me goodbye? Who is supposed to pay the bills?" (I had a job, but I was saving for a vehicle.)

On one end, I felt abandoned. I was confused. I was hurt. I didn't know what to do. On the other end, I felt happy, excited, 'GROWN!' Six hours later, my mother called me and said, "I know you will be OK. Remember what I've taught you. If you feel like it's too much, just move with your sister in College Station."

This experience changed my whole life. I started to think about myself differently since I had my own house as a senior in high school. I started dressing for school differently.

My favorite attire was suits. People used to ask me why I wore suits to school. I always replied, "I wear suits because I'm dressing to where I'm going." Or I would say, "I represent God, so I must dress my best." I stopped carrying a backpack and started carrying a briefcase. My mind was made up that I was going to be successful.

I was so FOCUSED that I joined the Texas Army National Guard a month after my mother left. Even though I was still in school, I attended drill weekends in Brenham, Texas.

After graduating from high school, I went on to basic training in Fort Benning, Georgia, and became a squad leader. I attended AIT (Advanced Individual Training) in Fort Lee, Virginia, and became the PG (Platoon Guild) and the Student First Sergeant.

When I completed my training, I ended up in Electra, TX, and started working for Wright Brand Foods in Vernon, TX.

After three months, I moved into my apartment and finally bought my first car. This car was a brand-new 2002 Ford Focus. I didn't have to acquire a cosigner to buy it, and I didn't have a high interest rate on the loan. It was delivered to me from Lubbock, TX.

I was only 19 years old when this happened. Two years later, I bought my first home without a cosigner. I was the first child under my grandparents to own a home. My grandparents had eight children and 27 grandchildren. I was the 8th grandchild!

I'm not telling you this story to impress you; I am telling you this story to impress upon you that it was my mother's teaching and the teaching of people I purposed to follow that helped me to make the right decisions in life.

I owe a lot to my mother, even though you may think she was wrong for leaving me to pay the bills while in high school. Here is a quote from the Bible that helped me understand my situation: "Be strong and courageous. Do not be afraid or terrified because of them, for the Lord your God goes with you; He will never leave you nor forsake you" (Deuteronomy 31:6). It's through my hardships in life that I became who I am today. I don't regret anything.

So far in this book, you have learned two things: The first is how to find the WHY that will make you responsible. The second is to remember that God created you to solve a problem for Him. Now, the third thing is to learn how to EMBRACE YOUR MENTOR'S MENTALITY.

It's time to R.E.S.E.T.

It is not wrong to go back to that which you have forgotten.
–West-African proverb

God

Genesis 1:1 says, "In the beginning, God ..." The word 'GOD' means Creator! In Hebrew, it's a singular plural name referenced as the Godhead, aka Trinity. That is why in Genesis 1:26, the Bible says, "Let 'Us' make man in 'Our' image and into 'Our' likeness."

Throughout the Bible, as you read, you will find out that God has many names. According to christiananswers.net, it's recorded that God has over 900 titles. Every name represents characteristics of God as well as His character. An attribute describes a specific trait or feature of Him.

God's character describes a group of attributes. For example, the Bible says that God is love (1 John 4:8). His characteristics of love is YHWH-Yireh, which means "The Lord will provide" (Genesis 22:14), or YHWH-Rapha, which means "The Lord that healeth" (Exodus 15:26), or YHWH-

Shalom, which means "The Lord our Peace" (Judges 6:24), or YHWH-Ra-ah, which means "The Lord my Shepherd" (Psalm 23:1), or YHWH-Nissi, which means "The Lord our Banner" (Exodus 17:8–15).

God gave us information about Him so we can discover who we are and how we should live. The Bible indicates that we were made in His image and into His likeness. The Bible is a book of instructions on how we should live our life. In fact (thank you, Pastor Early Williams III), the acronym HOLY BIBLE stands for "He Only Left You Basic Instruction Before Leaving Earth." My mentor Dr. Stan Harris says that the acronym BIBLE stands for "Breakthrough Insights Bringing Life Enrichments."

We must take hold of the instructions God has given us, let go of our EGO (Edging God Out, Edging Guidance Out), realizing that God is the only One that can raise our EGO (Edging Greatness Out). Embracing your mentor's mentality gives you leverage. John Paul Getty said, "I would rather earn 1% of the effort of 100 people than 100% of my efforts."

There are five different forms of leverage that we can take advantage of:

1. OPI- Other People's Ideas
2. OPT- Other People's Time
3. OPE- Other People's Experiences

4. OPM- Other People's Money
5. OPW- Other People's Work

How can you take advantage of the five forms of leverage? Let me spell it out for you: READ! When you READ, you Receive Empowerment, Authority, and Dominion. David Bailey said, "The best advice I ever got was that knowledge is power and to keep reading."

God Encourages Us to Study the Bible

John 5:39 says, "You study the Scriptures diligently because you think that in them you have eternal life. These are the very Scriptures that testify about me." Joshua 1:8 says, "This book of the law shall not depart out of thy mouth; but thou shalt meditate therein day and night, that thou mayest observe to do according to all that is written therein: for then thou shalt make thy way prosperous, and then thou shalt have GOOD SUCCESS."

God also instructs us to seek advice from multiple sources. Proverbs 11:14 says, "Where no counsel is, the people fall: but in the multitude of counselors, there is safety." My mentor the late Dr. Myles Munroe said, "If you want to be wise, keep company with wise men."

God warns us about what would happen if we don't seek out knowledge. Hosea 4:6 says, "My people are destroyed for lack of knowledge. And because you have rejected knowledge, I will reject you and ignore your children." When I first read that, I was like, "God, why would You ignore the children?" And God said, "Simple. If the parents don't find out the truth, how will the kids know?"

Parents will only teach their children what they know about life; therefore, it's not saying that God will reject the children. He said He's going to ignore them until they come up to a Jesus moment. And everybody knows how hard it is when you try to come up to your own Jesus moment. Most of the time, you will have to face your Jesus Moment when the mistake has already been made. I use the term 'a Jesus moment' from the story of the Prodigal Son. When he hit rock bottom in the hog pen, the Bible indicates that HE CAME TO HIMSELF (a Jesus moment) to change his situation (see Luke 15:16–17).

Priestly Role Model

A priestly role model is a parent who inspires their children to follow Christ by demonstrating how Christ has changed their own lives. The second thing our children crave is ADVICE.

God has instructed us to train our "child in the way he should go, and when he is old, he will not depart from it"

(Proverbs 22:6). Before we received Jesus Christ as our Lord and Savior, our first mentor was our parent(s).

It's the parents' job to teach the children who Christ is, His love and mercy, and His principles to live a prosperous life. God revealed to me that there is more than one way to reach an individual on their level of understanding. In 1 Corinthians 9:20, Paul said that to a Jew, he became a Jew that he might win Jews. In verse 22, he said, "I become all things to all men so though I may win some" (paraphasia added).

Now check this out: Albert Einstein said something about solving problems. He said, "We cannot solve our problems with the same thinking we used when we created them." WAIT! PAUSE, REWIND, AND PLAY! I said that Albert Einstein said, "We cannot solve our problems with the same thinking we used when we created them." Our mind must expand to find answers to our problems.

Have you noticed that I use acronyms in this book? I use them to convey the message so that you can understand a concept better. You must find different methods to teach your child the ways of God on their level of understanding.

Become Brilliant with the Basics

When Vince Lombardi took over the Green Bay Packers, the reporters asked him, "What are you going to do differently as the new head coach?" Vince Lombardi said,

"The same guys will play. We will use the same style of offense and defense. The only difference is, we will become brilliant with the basics."

I use this same "become brilliant with the basics" principle to teach my daughters how Christ changed my life. 2 Chronicles 7:14 says, "If My people, which are called by My name, shall humble themselves, and pray, and seek My face, and turn from their wicked ways; then will I hear from Heaven, and will forgive their sin, and will heal their land." This Scripture is the basic teaching for a person to follow Christ.

I use the words 'humble themselves, pray, seek his face, turn from their wicked ways' as the foundation to teach about God and His principles. I share my life stories and examples from the Bible to convey a message. I found that your own life stories are very effective because you have actually experienced it, and you will be able to deliver the message with full conviction.

Humble Thyself

The phrase 'humble thyself' means to "be brought down." In other words, bring yourself under authority. The Bible should be the first and last place we look for answers.

I tell my daughters all the time that as females, there is a way to conduct themselves because people already have a negative image of them. Therefore, HOW THEY DRESS DETERMINES HOW THEY WANT TO BE ADDRESSED!

I educate my daughters about their clothing attire. I explain that a person can know a lot about another person just by the clothes they wear. I explain to them that if they wear certain clothing, they will attract a certain breed of men. Proverbs 31:25 says, "She is clothed with strength and dignity; she can laugh at the days to come."

Whenever we are in public, and we see women wearing revealing clothing, I stop doing what I was doing to give them a teaching moment. I ask them, "What is wrong with this picture?" They always say, "Her clothes! She needs to put on different clothes." I then say, "If you don't respect yourself through the clothing you wear, how do you expect other people to respect you?"

I also talk to my daughters about relationships. Most relationships nowadays are based on money and sex. So, I tell them, "You don't need a man in your life for money. You can make your own money. In fact, YOU MUST HAVE A LIFE BEFORE YOU BECOME SOMEONE'S WIFE."

The only reason why a person wants a relationship is for companionship. And if people don't have their life straight, then they don't need a relationship. Adam was operating in his purpose before God gave him Eve (Genesis 2:17–25). In fact, Adam didn't know he needed a mate until God brought Eve to him.

I explain to my daughters that if they fully depend on the man's income in order to live, they would feel obligated to stay in the relationship even when it goes sour—because they need financial support.

When an evil man knows you don't have anywhere to go, he will then abuse you emotionally, physically, and financially. But when you make your own money, your confidence will kick in, and you may even say "I can do bad all by myself" and leave.

It is essential that all parents who are reading this book talk to their children about sex. Sex isn't a dirty word! I talk about sex with my children all the time. I rather for them to hear from me than to listen on the streets. If they hear it from me first, then they will receive the truth. If they hear from the streets first, they won't receive the whole truth.

My daughters and I started talking about this subject when they started on their first menstrual cycle. I explain to them that their bodies are the temple of the Holy Spirit. God made their bodies to bear children. In essence, a woman is a multiplier:

If you give a woman a house, she will turn the house into a home.

If you give a woman grocery, she will turn the grocery into a meal.

If you give a woman sperm, she will turn the sperm into a baby.

If you give a woman trouble, she will turn the trouble into HELL!!!

Lol.

Let your children see you read the Bible. In fact, read the Bible together as a family. Hold Bible study in the home and answer questions about things that may be unclear to them.

Pray

This word 'Pray' means to petition to a supernatural being, aka GOD. I teach prayer using an experience where I had no choice but to pray to receive the answer. I told my children that my mentor Dr. Stan Harris called me one day and said, "Willie, have you heard of a company called XYZ?" I said, "No." He then said, "Well, I want you to purchase a package to learn about this new technology. In return, you will have an opportunity to set yourself and your family up financially." I said, "OK, I want to purchase a small package first. How much is that?" He said, "Around $600."

About a month later, I saw I had made my money back. I then went to my wife and explained to her what had happened. She asked, "How much for the biggest package?" I said to her, "The biggest package is $15,000." She said, "Let's go big, or let's go home!" By the way, this was the first time my wife would agree to any entrepreneur adventure I went for in the past. So, for some reason, the BEAST came out of me when she said: "Let's go big, or let's go home!" I asked her how much we had in our emergency fund, and she said, "$4,000." I didn't know how I was going to get the remaining amount.

I went back to my mentor and said, "Dr. Stan, I don't know where I can get the remaining amount to purchase the biggest package." Dr. Stan said, "Whenever you can't figure out something, I want you to say this to yourself: 'When I make up my mind to do something, God will orchestrate circumstances to align themselves in my favor. When I say I can't, my mind stops trying, but when I ask, *How can I?* my mind keeps searching until it finds a way. There is a way, and I will find it. If not by the grace of God, I will invite it.'"

It took me 30 minutes to digest Dr. Stan's words. I probably said it to myself over 100 times. The following day, I prayed to God and said, "God, open my eyes! What am I missing, Lord?" Then BAM!!! God said to me, "Stand still and don't say anything." So, I stopped talking and started listening.

God asked me, "Do you remember the conversation I had with Moses?" I took my Bible and went to Exodus chapters 3 and 4. I started reading about Moses, where he was complaining to God, saying he's not the man for the job. When he was done complaining, God stepped in and said something powerful. God said, "What is that in your hand?" For Moses, it was a staff, and that staff helped deliver God's people from Pharaoh.

God said to me, "What is in your hand? What is in your possession that will help you get the job done?" I said, "I don't know, God." God intervened again and said, "Dr. Stan Harris taught you the bank-to-bank principle a couple of months ago, right?" I replied, "Yes, I remember." God said again to me, "What is in your hand? What is in your possession?" (Side note: The bank-to-bank principle is when you take money that's going down in value and invest it in something that is going up in value and then use the money that's going up in value to pay off the loan.)

Then it hit me! I had two paid-off vehicles! I went to the bank and received a loan on the cars. Within 24 hours of saying that prayer/affirmation, I was able to find the money, and I purchased the package. I can't tell you how much money I made because you won't believe me.

Teaching your children how to pray will position them for success. There will be times when they will have nobody to talk to or depend on. Show them how important prayer is by demonstrating your prayer life. My acronym PRAYER is Presenting Request And Yielding Expecting Results.

Seek His Face

The phrase 'seek his face' refers to God's presence. I teach God's presence through a principle I learned from my mother. My mother said, "If you live with someone, make sure you make them mad when you leave." I didn't understand it at first, but it made sense after she explained it. She was talking about bringing so much value into the environment that people will notice a change in the environment when you leave. This will cause them to be mad because you are gone. I use this principle while working on a paid internship. I use it while in church. I use it everywhere I go.

I witnessed the power of this principle when I left the military after 13 years of service. My unit held a goodbye ceremony for soldiers who had ETS (Expiration of Term of Service). It was September 2013, drill weekend. We all had to say a speech of farewell and encouragement. After my speech, my platoon sergeant, SFC Chrishelle Mckenzie, started crying, and when I saw her, I started crying too because it hurt me to see her cry. I hugged her and thanked her for changing my life.

God's presence will always make the environment better. Without the presence of God, a person cannot function correctly. You will learn more about that later.

Turn Away from Your Wicked Ways

The phrase 'Turn away from your wicked ways' references God's Holy Spirit convicting you to change. The Holy Spirit will also convict you while you're in the moment of sinning. I taught this principle to my kids by telling them about an experience I had as a 15-year-old.

I was living in College Station, TX, at that time, and it was Halloween. My cousin Larry Smith said, "Let's go to the Texas A&M college dorm rooms." I said, "OK, let's go!" It was night time, and we were able to get inside the dorms.

We started walking through the hallway, and we saw an expensive jam box sitting outside this particular dorm room. My cousin said, "Pick it up, Willie, and let's go." I picked it up, and we both started running. We made it to the end of the hallway. I stopped and said to my cousin, "I can't steal this. This is not me. I'm better than that!" I walked back to the dorm room and placed the jam box back in front of the door and walked home.

I told my children that it was God that stopped me in the hallway because God already instilled in me to not steal. Exodus 20:15 says, "You shall not steal."

Teach your children how important it is to grow with the Lord. Explain that following Christ makes a person better in every situation. A priestly role model is a parent who inspires their children to follow Christ by demonstrating how Christ has changed their own lives.

Change is the end result of all true learning.
– Leo Buscaglia

Principles

1. Our life story was meant for us to share and inspire others.

2. A setback is a setup for a comeback.

3. To a child, the parents are their first mentor.

4. Parents must teach principles from God's Word.

5. Our children will suffer if we, as parents, refuse to grow in knowledge.

6. Parents must train at the level of the child's education.

7. Personal experiences are more convicting than other stories.

PRAYER

Father God, in the name of Jesus, we pray for guidance. We understand that You created us, and every manufacturer knows everything about their product. We ask You to teach us life principles so we can teach our children. Thank You for making our mess into a message. Continue to guide us to be the world-class parents that You designed us to be. In Jesus' name. Amen.

Questions

1. Can you remember a particular time in your life you thought it was the end of the world, but later, you realized it was a life lesson for you to share to help others? Explain.

2. What are some ways you can keep learning principles to allow yourself to prosper as a parent?

3. Why is telling your story so important?

CHAPTER FOUR

Set Your Ideal Work Environment

We make the world we live in and shape our own environment.
−Orison Swett Marden

The Right Environment

Mel: "10 to 6!"

Me: "This is 6. Go ahead!"

Mel: "Willie, where is your location?"

Me: "I'm currently placing labels on the bags in the room next to the MCC. Is this Mel?"

Mel: "Yes, this is Mel." [She opened the door.] "Hello, Willie, I have two auditors here wanting to ask you a couple of questions about quality."

Me: "Sure! How can I help you today?"

Auditor 1: "Hello, Willie, I'm Dorothy."

Me: "Hello, Dorothy, it's nice to meet you."

Dorothy: "I only have one question to ask you."
Me: "OK."

Dorothy: "What are the different systems in place for quality control to communicate the quality of the product being produced?"

Me: "Well, Dorothy, we have many systems of communicating quality in place. We have email, safety meetings, the radio, and communication boards. If Mel has something that we needed to talk ASAP, she will call me up to her office."

Dorothy: "Thank you, Willie! That's all I need to ask."

Sam (2nd auditor): "I know you are ready to go home to get some sleep."

Me: "Yes, I am, but I can't go to sleep just yet. I have to finish writing a chapter in my book."

Sam: "I saw your book cover on your desk."

Me: "It's the manuscript for my book. The book cover will be the actual book cover I will use for the paperback."

Sam: "Tell me, what is your book about?"

Me: "The name of my book is: *Press the RESET Button: My Journey from Being a Fatherless Child to a World-Class Parent*."

Sam: "Sounds very interesting …"

Dorothy: "I can't see myself writing a book."

Me: "You know what, Dorothy? I said the same thing until I started hanging around great people, people that believe in you more than you will believe in yourself. I learned a long time ago from T. D. Jakes that if you're the most significant person in your group, then you are in the wrong group. For some reason, successful people have a magical way of pulling the greatest out of you. Things I thought would be impossible for me to accomplish, I end up doing without any motivation and inspiration."

Sam: "Sounds great! Good luck with your journey."

ME: "Thank you, Sam and Dorothy, for stopping by."

Two years ago, I posted the book cover on Facebook. Everyone thought the book was out and wanted to buy it. What they didn't know is this: I posted it for myself. I needed motivation and inspiration to write it. The first year passed, and I didn't even write a single word. The second year passed, and still, not a word. Until January 12, 2018! My mentor Dr. Stan Harris called me and said, "I need you to be at this conference, and it's going to be tomorrow. Can you make it?" I told him, "Yes, I can make it."

When I arrived there, I knew I had stepped into a different environment. The RESET Conference was organized by Dr. Anne Kappel and Adele J. Foster-Glenn. They had a lineup of speakers to inspire and motivate everyone. Dr. Stan Harris, Dr. Kenisha Morton, Tacey Casey-Arnold, Sundiata Ferguson, and many more. The keynote speaker was the one and only Tawana Williams, aka The Hope Coach. I will tell you more about her later.

Anyway, after I left that conference, I was liberated and transformed. On the way back home, God began to speak to me like He never did before. He said, "I want you to use the RESET philosophy to motivate and educate the world on how to become unstoppable in achieving any goal they set for themselves."

The next Sunday, I preached a sermon titled "Press the RESET Button." I know this happened because the environment of the RESET Conference triggered my greatest to come forth. In other words, I was pregnant, and my water broke.

So far in this book, you have learned three things: The first is how to find the WHY that will make you responsible. The second is to remember that God created you to solve a problem for Him. The third is to embrace your mentor's mentality. Now, the fourth thing to learn is how to SET YOUR IDEAL WORK ENVIRONMENT. If you are ready,

It's time to R.E.S.E.T.

You have to believe in yourself that you can do anything, and you have to believe in God. BELIEVE: Because Emmanuel Lives, I Expect Victory Every time.
–Willie Tubbs

HEAVENS ...

Genesis 1:1 says, "God created the Heavens ..." I asked God why He created the Heavens. God went ahead to explain to me that He always establishes the environment of the product so that the product can function correctly:

- God created the heavens so that the earth can function correctly.

- God created the atmosphere, so the fowls of the earth can function correctly.

- God created the waters so that the sea animals can function correctly.

- God created the land so that land animals can function correctly.

- God planted a garden called Eden so that humans can function correctly.

The word 'function' deals with being able to fulfill destiny. The earth cannot fulfill its destiny if it doesn't rotate in space. The fowls of the earth cannot fulfill their destiny if they don't fly in the air. The sea animals cannot fulfill their destiny if they don't have water to live in. The land animals cannot fulfill their destiny if they don't have land to live on. Humans cannot fulfill their destiny if they don't have Eden to live in.

God could have placed Adam anywhere on earth, but He decided to place him in Eden. Why? After studying what the word 'Eden' means in the Ancient Hebrew language, I realized that it's not just a place; it's also the presence of God. If you read Genesis chapters 1 to 3, you would notice that Adam never prayed to God. Adam never had to sacrifice an animal to be worthy of God's presence. God walked in the garden in the cool of the day (Genesis 3:8).

God warned Adam and Eve that if they ate the fruit of good and evil, they would die. When they committed treason against God, they were placed outside the Garden of Eden. And the first thing that happened while outside the Garden of Eden was the first case of domestic violence. Kane killed Abel!

Throughout the Bible, you will see man's attempt to find himself back into the presence of God until Jesus Christ, the second Adam (1 Corinthians 15:45) came into the scene to put everything back into its proper perspective. If it weren't for the death of Christ, we wouldn't have the opportunity to be forgiven of our sins (Matthew 26:28). So, now, we have the chance to come back to Eden (the presence of God).

I'm going to explain it like this: When a manufacturer produces a product, they will embed the laws of limitations within the product. For example, can anyone use a hair dryer while taking a shower? The answer is: "No! It will malfunction." But why? The hairdryer wasn't designed to be in that kind of environment. In essence, we weren't intended to be outside Eden (the presence of God). If you don't have God's presence in your life, you are actually malfunctioning.

Before the fall of man, we entered into God's presence naturally. Now, we have to work to be in the presence of God. The psalmist said, "This is the day the Lord has made; I will rejoice and be glad in it" (Psalm 118:24). David had to activate his will by deciding to praise God to be in His presence.

Philippians 4:8 says, "Finally, brethren, whatsoever things are true, whatsoever things are honest, whatsoever things are just, whatsoever things are pure, whatsoever things are lovely, whatsoever things are of good report; if there be any virtue, and if there be any praise, think on these things." Here, God is literally telling us how to be in His presence. It starts with your **MIND**!

Being in His presence gives you the opportunity to work efficiently. I always say, "A flower can still bloom in the desert, but if the flower stays in the desert, it becomes dead like the desert." Therefore, the flower must uproot itself from that environment and find a setting that contributes to its greatness instead of a setting that is detrimental to its growth.

Positive Role Model

A positive role model is a parent who inspires their children to have a positive mentality by demonstrating how a positive mentality is affecting them. The third thing our children crave is ADORATION.

As parents, we must provide an environment that gives our children the opportunity to reach their full potential and greatness. If parents don't provide a conducive climate for growth and transformation, the children will look outside the house to search for it. Therefore, parents have to set the tone to provide a positive vibe in the whole house.

The Power of Words

One day, I asked my oldest daughter, Ashanti, to dance with me. She replied, "I can't." I told her, "Don't speak the word *can't*." She then asked me, "Why, Daddy?" I began to explain how human beings operate.

The first thing I told her is this: "We all came into this world with an open mind. In other words, we learn from watching, reading, and listening. The three gates of learning frame how we think. How we think determines how we feel. How we feel determines what decisions we make. Our choices determine our actions. Our actions establish our habits. Our habits determine our destiny.

"If your response is that you can't dance, then we must look at why you made that decision. To know why you made that kind of choice, we must first understand how you were feeling. To understand how you were feeling, we must first understand what you were thinking. To know how you were thinking, we must first understand what words you're listening to—which will shape your belief system."

"I didn't know that," my daughter said.

"I have more to tell you," I said. "Our brain has two dimensions. We have a conscious mind and a subconscious mind. Our conscious mind is active when we consciously think about something. This is where the three gates of learning are located. For example, if I say, 'DON'T think of a BLUE balloon,' what just happened? A person will see in their mind's eye a blue balloon.

"Our subconscious mind is active when you do things automatically, without conscious thought. This is where your belief system and memories are located. For example, if you were like a deer in the headlights the last time you gave a speech, chances are you will replay that same memory in your mind over and over. Eventually, your belief system will determine if you will ever speak in front of people again—because of your experience.

"To understand how the conscious and subconscious work together, you have to follow the captain and crew analogy. The captain is the conscious mind, and the crew is the subconscious mind. The captain (the 3 gates of learning) is in control of the ship. If the captain tells the crew to row right, the crew will row to the right. If the captain tells the crew to row left, the crew will row to the left.

"Now, do you remember a game called telephone? The telephone is a game involving five or more people in a line. The objective of the game is to whisper a phrase or word to the person next to you. When the message makes it to the last person, he or she says what was said to them. Nine times out of ten, the message is entirely different from when it was first told. In essence, when the message is delivered from the captain to the crew, the captain will have to say the news more than one time to make sure everyone receives the message. That's why the Bible says, 'Faith comes by hearing and hearing by the word of God' (Romans 10:17).

"In the meantime, while the crew members are directed to go left and right, they don't know if they are going the right way. Remember, the crew is the subconscious mind. This is where memories and your belief system are located. If the captain thinks and feels they won't make it to the land safely, then the crew won't believe or act as if they can make it to the land safely.

"Now, check this out: If the captain receives a radio call from another ship that has already made it to the land safely, saying, 'You can make it; just keep going,' the captain will report to the crew, 'Keep rowing. I just got word: the storm is clearing up.' The crew will act on the belief that the storm is clearing up."

As parents, we must be the voice on the radio encouraging our children to pursue that very thing that may seem too hard to go through. We must set an environment that will make our children believe all things are possible.

If we tell our children that they will never be anything in their life, and we keep saying it, pretty soon those words will get down in their subconscious mind, and once they believe it, their belief system will be hard to change. The Bible says that we would be transformed by the renewing of the mind (Romans 12:2).

When my daughters do something they know I don't approve of, I use an effective communication formula I learned from my mentor's wife, Mrs. Nadia Harris. She said, "LOVE, LISTEN, DISCERN, then RESPOND." I always say to my daughters, "First, I love you, and you mean the world to me. But I hate that you decided to do this. And now, I have to discipline you to help you remember I love you, sweetie ..."

The Bible says that life and death are in the power of the tongue (Proverbs 18:21). Have you ever monitored your words? Do you believe in yourself? Do you feel DOUBT (Depending On Understanding Before Trusting) creeping into your mind, trying to dismantle your belief system?

We must watch what we say to our children. We must watch what we do around our children. We must watch what they say about themselves. Learning this one principle will bring your home environment into a realm of focused intention for success.

Personal Development

I'm an avid reader. Reading personal development books changed my belief system. I told my two daughters, two nieces, and two nephews that I have an idea to help them to make some extra money. I told them I would pay them 20 dollars for every book they read. The catch is that I have to pick the book, and if they read a book every week, they will receive 100 dollars a month. They all agreed ...

I pay my family to read personal development books. Personal development is one of the best ways to program a positive mental attitude. The Bible says, "For lack of guidance a nation falls, but victory is won through many advisers" (Proverbs 11:14, NIV).

Learning how people overcame certain situations and reading motivation, inspirational, and informational books, articles, and poems will give a person HOPE (Help Other People Excel) to continue to walk in FAITH (Forward Action In The Hope).

Here are two AWESOME poems my daughters and I say to ourselves that catapult us into a BEASTMODE mentality: "OUR DEEPEST FEAR" by Marianne Williamson and "My Daily Attitude Adjuster" by Dr. Stan Harris.

OUR DEEPEST FEAR by Marianne Williamson

Our deepest fear is not that we are inadequate. Our deepest fear is that we are strong and powerful beyond measure. It is our light, not our darkness that frightens us. We ask ourselves, *Who am I to be gorgeous, beautiful, intelligent, and fabulous?* Actually, who are you not to be? You are a child of God. You're playing small does not serve the world. There is nothing in life about shrinking so that other people won't feel insecure around you. You were meant to shine as children do. We were born to manifest through the glory of God that is within us. It's not just in some of us; it's in all of us. And when we let our light shine so brightly, we unconsciously give other people the permission to do the same because, as we are liberated from our own fear, our presence automatically liberates others. Our deepest fear.

My Daily Attitude Adjuster by Dr. Stan Harris

Wow! What a great day to be alive. I feel dynamite. I like me. I accept me. I love me. I'm going to have a super fantastic day today because I'm too blessed to be depressed. I'm too blessed to be stressed. I'm too glad to be sad. I'm too anointed to be disappointed. And I'm too elated to be agitated. Circumstances are aligning themselves in my favor. I'm healthy, physically fit, and intellectually equipped. I have wisdom far beyond my years. I am an extraordinary person with incredible abilities that I will use to add value to others' lives—because I know that as I help others reach their dreams, I will automatically reach my own.

I anticipate meeting the person or group of people today who are willing to use their power, their wealth and influence to help me achieve my dreams. All day long, people will go out of their way to bless me. Today, I will add a significant value to somebody's life. I will show compassion to those in need. I will give strength to the weak and inspiration to the weary. Someone needs what I have to offer, and I gladly make myself available.

I embrace abundance, and it embraces me. I am abundant in every good way. I am an abundance magnet. I like money, and it likes me. It is attracted to me because it comes abundantly from many sources. I use my money wisely because it's a tool to help those in need. It's also a way of keeping score, showing how many people's lives I added value to. I am experiencing great victories, supernatural turnarounds and miraculous breakthroughs in the midst of great impossibilities.

I am an overcomer. If my mountain can't be removed, I will develop and practice my mountain-climbing skills. I may experience a setback. Setbacks are only setups for comebacks. Setbacks pave the way for comebacks. I will make lemonade out of life's lemons. And if life knocks me down, I'll follow my back, realizing that as long as I can look up, I can get up. I commit to paying for my dreams with preparation and perspiration so that I won't have to live with nightmares of regret.

I do not procrastinate—because procrastination leads to devastation. It is the assassination of my destination; thus, I will act now. I am a doer. I get results that last. I now release the champion that is inside of me. I am the leader that multitudes of people are looking for. I choose to succeed today and every day hereafter. Watch out, world, here I come.

Role models really matter. It's hard to imagine yourself as something you don't see.
—Chelsea Clinton

Gratitude

Serving in the military has granted me the privilege to go to Iraq for a year. I say privilege because Iraq is where my relationship with God became intimate. One day, I was traveling from Camp Bucca to Camp Tallil, I saw 3 Iranian kids playing in the front of their home. They were laughing, having a great time.

God: "Do you see how much fun they are having?"

Me: "Yes."

God: "What is the temperature for today?"

Me: "145 degrees."

God: "Where is their restroom?"

Me: "Outside."
God: "Look real close at their legs and tell me what you see."

Me: "Are you serious! They don't have any shoes on!"

God: "Remember what you are experiencing right now. I want you to tell everyone what you have seen."

That moment changed my whole life. I realized how blessed we are in the United States. We take so much stuff for granted and we complain about the craziest things. I made it my business to go home and teach my children about the importance of gratitude.

Every day, I told them to write ten things that they are grateful for. Each day, they had to write something different because I wanted them to really think. After seven days, we would start the process over again. This changed their attitudes and mine. I really suggest you and your family try this practice.

A positive role model is a parent who inspires their children to have a positive mentality by demonstrating how a positive mentality is affecting them.

"Acknowledging the good that you already have in your life is the foundation for all abundance." -Eckhart Tolle

Principles

1. If you're the most significant person in your group, then you are in the wrong group.

2. Great people will believe in you more than you will believe in yourself.

3. Without Eden, we cannot fulfill our destiny.

4. If parents don't give a productive climate for growth and transformation, children will look outside the house to search for it.

5. Your life follows your words.

6. Positive affirmation sets the tone for you as well as your environment.

7. Personal development changes your belief system.

Prayer

Father God, in the name of Jesus, You have given us Your presence to make sure we fulfill our destiny. Thank You for Your presence, God. I don't want to go anywhere without Your presence. I don't want to go to work, church, or be in the presence of children without Your presence. I don't want to malfunction as a human being, especially as a parent. So, in the name of Jesus, You said this is the day the Lord has made; I will rejoice and be glad in it. Let us, Father, into your presence right now. In Jesus' name. Amen.

Questions

1. Who are the people in your life you need to cut off?

2. Are you the most significant person in your circle? If yes, what can you do to attract more influencers into your life?

CHAPTER FIVE

Employ Yourself and Your Resources

Our uniqueness, our individuality, and our life experiences mold us into fascinating beings. I hope we can embrace that. I pray we may all challenge ourselves to delve into the deepest resources of our hearts to cultivate an atmosphere of understanding, acceptance, tolerance, and compassion. We are all in this life together.
–Linda Thompson

I can do all THINGS

"Hello, my name is Tawana Williams, and I was blessed to be born without arms and impaired use of my legs due to the drug thalidomide that was given to my mother when she was pregnant with me."

I looked up, and I said to myself, *This is the one and only Tawana Williams*. She went on to say that her mother told her that there was nothing she could not do. "I also had a grandma Rogers that did not play with me. When I was four and a half years old, she looked me in the eyes and said: 'Tee, you must not need arms because God didn't give it to you.' She said, 'Nothing is missing; if you don't have it, you don't need it.'"

As Tawana Williams continued to speak, tears started flowing down my eyes. This woman was gang-raped, raped by her stepfather, addicted to crack and cocaine for ten years. She experienced abortion, motherhood, a stroke, and a mild heart attack. She is a living testimony of how to be unarmed but dangerous! Now, she is a MOTIVATIONAL SPEAKER, AUTHOR, ARTIST, TV PERSONALITY, ADVOCATE, MENTOR, EXECUTIVE PRODUCER, BUSINESS WOMAN, HUMANITARIAN & CEO! She is called the Hope Coach.

After Tawana Williams was done speaking, she stood up and started singing "I won't complain," and everybody at the RESET Conference started crying. Tears fell down her face as she was singing. I knew there was a shift in mindset to believe that 2018 was my year to blossom. It was Tawana Williams's testimony that stopped me dead in my tracks to say, "No more excuses!"

So far in this book, you have learned three things: The first is how to find the WHY that will make you responsible. The second is to remember that God created you to solve a problem for Him. The third is to embrace your mentor's mentality. The fourth is to set your ideal work environment. Now the fifth thing is to learn how to EMPLOY YOURSELF AND YOUR RESOURCES.

It's time to R.E.S.E.T.

Your past has brought you to your present, change your present, and you change your future.
–Keither Williams 'Toby'

and the Earth ...

Genesis 1:1 says, "In the beginning, God created the Heavens and the earth."

Now, check this out!

The reason you picked up this book is that you were searching to answer the five questions of life. There are over seven billion people on this earth trying to answer these questions.

These questions control everything we do. These questions control our environment. These questions control our health. These questions control our economy. These questions answer why a young person will get involved in a gang. These questions also answer why a person would join a golf club or fish all day long. These questions are the reason why you woke up this morning. These questions are the reason why you go to a job that you hate. These questions are the reason why you brush your teeth every morning. These questions are the reason why you want to rescue yourself and lead your children to their greatness. Do you want to know what these questions are?

The first question is, why am I here? This is a question of purpose. If you noticed, I answered this question in chapter 2. In that chapter , I explained why God started our beginning—because He wanted us to exist alongside Him in eternity, but in a different place called earth, to solve a problem for Him. As for parents, the answer to the 'why am I here' question is to become a Purposed Role Model.

The second and third questions of life are, who am I and where do I come from? These are questions of Identity and Heritage. In chapter 3, I stated that the Bible is a book of instructions on how we should live our life.

All manufacturers will always give a book of instructions with the product to make sure the customer fully understands the product. In this case, the book of instructions is called the Bible. Genesis 1:26 says, "Then

God said, 'Let us make mankind in our image, in our likeness, so that they may rule over the fish in the sea and the birds in the sky, over the livestock and all the wild animals, [a] and over all the creatures that move along the ground.'" And Psalm 82:6 says, "I said, 'You are "gods"; you are all sons of the Most-High.'" As for parents, the answer to the 'who am I and where do I come from' questions is, become a Priestly Role Model.

The fourth question of life is, what can I do? This is a question of Potential. In chapter 4, I stated that God always creates the environment of the product so that the product can function correctly. You will never know if you can fully reach your greatness if you are in the wrong environment. Do you remember the analogy of the hair dryer? As for parents, the answer the 'what can I do' question is, become a Positive Role Model.

The last question of life is, where am I going? This is a question of Destiny. Human beings were the final thing God wanted to create He went to the ground to form man. Genesis 2:7 says, "The Lord God formed man from the dust of the ground and breathed into him, into his nostril, the breath of life. And man became a living thing."

God took what He had to get what He wanted. In other words, God employed His resources to make man. When God touched the ground to make man, He was showing that He is a practical God.

When Jesus came down to the earth, God furthermore demonstrated how practical He is. As for parents, the answer to the 'where am I going' question is, become a Practical Role Model.

God knew we weren't going to fix the sin problem. So He sent His son to the earth to redeem us. While Jesus Christ was reclaiming us, He answered the purpose, identity, heritage, potential, and destiny questions. For Jesus Christ to answer these questions, He went through adversity. John 16:33 says, "These things I have spoken unto you, that in me ye might have peace. In the world ye shall have tribulation: but be of good cheer; I have overcome the world."

Practical Role Model

A practical role model is a parent who inspires their children to overcome adversity by demonstrating how they overcame adversity. The fourth thing our children crave is AFFECTION.

It is important to show our children our wounds. We must show them where we have failed and how we overcame it. We demonstrate this by employing our resources to convey a message of transformation, encouragement, and LOVE. So, we can give them HOPE (Help Other People Excel) whenever they fall into adversity.

Don't Let the School System Label Your Child

I just finished preaching the "Press the RESET Button" message, and everyone was heading home. My family jumped into the car to go home.

I said, "Ashanti and Vatanie, tell me the truth; how did Daddy do?" Every time I speak, I always ask my two judges how I did.

"You did great, Daddy," Ashanti said.

"You did very well, Daddy," Vatanie said.

Then I asked them on a scale of 1–10 how I did.

"I will give you a 9," Ashanti said.

"I will give you a 7," Vatanie said.

"What do I need to improve on, Vatanie?" I asked.

"Daddy, I notice you start stuttering a little when you get too excited," Vatanie said.

"Yeah, I notice that too," Ashanti jumped in.

"OK, I'm going to work on that. What did you like most about the message?" I asked.

"I loved the fact you mentioned: 'Don't let the school system label your children,'" Ashanti said.

On hearing the above, my heart melted. In the first chapter, I talked about my experience with my teacher in the 2nd grade. That one experience was the beginning of a long journey of feeling incompetent. Not knowing I was Dyslexic and having ADD until last year (2017), I now see why learning was so hard for me. Still, to this day, it's difficult for me to read out loud. I barely made it out of high school.

My classmates didn't know because I was so focused on success. I started businesses after businesses. I failed so many times that my co-workers laughed at me. They would ask, "Have you become a millionaire yet?" Or when I say "This is my last year at this place," they would respond by saying, "You said that last year, Willie." Now, I'm becoming a very successful entrepreneur. 35 years wise, and this would be my last year working for anybody else. I'm telling you my story because your story matters. You never know who needs to hear it.

Adversity causes some men to break; others to break records.
–William Arthur Ward

I told the story of my school experience to my children a long time ago. Knowing my daughter, Ashanti was suffering. She would bring home horrible grades from school. Vatanie has always been my straight-A student. But Ashanti struggled, and when Ladonna and I saw this, we decided to get our baby some help.

So, we set a meeting with Sylvan Learning Center to see if we could figure out the problem. They tested her and found out that nothing was wrong. They said she was where she needed to be. My wife and I were confused because we saw her struggle in school.

At times, she didn't want us to see her report card, and yes, we did go to the school to talk to her teachers. We continued to work with her at home through projects and homework. I even started searching online for answers. In the meantime, we continually reassured her that there was nothing wrong with her, and we loved her so much. WE WOULD FIND THE ANSWER!!!

One day, Ashanti said, "I'm going to be playing in the 6th-grade band this year. Can you buy me a flute?"

"OK, sweetie, let's go to Amazon.com to see how much it is," I said. As I scrolled down the page, I saw prices like $400, $300, $290. I said to Ashanti, "If I buy this, you will have to commit to this. I'm not just going to buy something, and you do not commit to it. Do you understand?"

"I know," she replied.

I called her sister, Vatanie, in the room and said, "Remember this: Whenever you to start something new, you may become discouraged at the beginning because you are learning something new. But EVERY MASTER WAS ONCE A MESS. THEREFORE, EVERY MESS CAN BE A MASTER!" I looked into their eyes and continued, "YOU HAVE TO BE COMMITTED TO THE PROCESS OF BEING BAD LONG ENOUGH UNTIL YOU CAN GET GOOD! THERE IS NOTHING YOU CAN'T DO! YOU CAN DO ALL THINGS THROUGH CHRIST WHO STRENGTHENS YOU."

"I've committed, Daddy!" Ashanti said.

I bought the flute, and boy let me tell you … not only was she determined, but she also exceeded my expectations. She practiced every day! She made the first chair in her first chair test. At home, after she had finished going over the music from school, she would go on YouTube to find new songs to play. Her grades went up, and eventually, she became an A & B student. She is an artist. Her grandmother taught her how to crochet. Everything just skyrocketed for her.

One day, after I made it home from work, as I lay in bed, I heard Ashanti playing the song "One Thousand Years" by Christina Perri on her flute. I got up and ran into her room and said with great excitement, "Sweetie, you are playing that song on your flute?"

She looked at me and said with a smile, "Yes, Daddy." I then looked at her and said, "You are awesome!" As tears rolled down my face, I said, "When I first bought this flute, you said that you were going to commit, but I didn't know how committed you were. Do you remember when I told you that you had to be committed?"

She said, "Yes! In fact, Daddy, you said I have to be committed to the process of being bad or feeling bad long enough until I can get good. Thank you for buying this flute for me."

You should never view your challenges as a disadvantage. Instead, it's important for you to understand that your experience facing and overcoming adversity is actually one of your biggest advantages.
–Michelle Obama

One Powerful Resource

A couple of years ago, when my wife and I were having a difficult time communicating, I heard about a book that was changing the lives of married couples—*The 5 Love Languages* by Gary Chapman.

I bought a copy for my wife, and I bought one for myself. And boy let me tell you, it changed my life. It talks about how we all have five different ways to communicate our love to each other, but there is a dominant language we prefer to use to express our appreciation.

One of the love languages is called 'Words of Affirmation.' People feel loved when a person is constantly saying words of encouragement, endearment, and appreciation.

'Time' is another love language. Some people feel loved when you spend quality time with them.

'Acts of Service' is another language. Some people feel loved when their spouse does things like fill up the gas tank or wash the clothes and dishes without them knowing.

'Physical Touch' is another love language. Some people feel loved when their spouse massages their back, holding hands, and snuggling.

'Gifts' is the last love language. Some people feel loved when their spouse surprises them with a gift.

We all use all five love languages to communicate our passion. The key is to find your spouse's dominant love language and use it 90% of the time. But also mix in the other love languages to spice the relationship up. This information helped me and my wife to understand each other better.

Our children have the five love languages too. As parents, we must identify their dominant love language and love them the way they want to be loved. Ashanti's dominant love language is 'Words of Affirmation.' Since we knew that, Ladonna and I kept speaking life in her while she was going through her situation in school. Now that she has overcome her adversity, I tell her that she is my shero for overcoming her situation.

Vatanie's dominant love language is 'Gifts.' She loves to be surprised with things my wife and I buy for her. Knowing your children's love language is also a great motivation tool to help them reach their potential. Our children need us to know how to love them through good times and bad times.

If you can give your child only one gift, let it be enthusiasm.
–Bruce Barton

Restoring Broken Relationships

Dr. Stan Harris told me about his relationship with his brother. Dr. Stan said he was on fire for God. Going all around the world, preaching. Speaking in all 50 states and several other countries around the world. Dr. Stan heard that all black men were lazy, so he made up his mind to prove everyone wrong. For 18 years, Dr. Stan was living off three to four hours of sleep a day until his body said enough is enough, and he collapsed.

Dr. Stan was so sick that his children had to help him up to go to the restroom. After several months, his health was better, and he ran into his brother. His brother said, "Don't take this wrong, but did you feel resistance in our relationship throughout the years?"

"Yes, I wondered why," Dr. Stan said.

"Don't take this wrong, but I was happy you got sick," his brother replied.

"EXCUSE ME?" Dr. Stan said, surprised.

"For a long time, I saw you saving souls for God. You were doing big things for yourself. I couldn't relate to you because I was always failing at everything. But when you became sick, I could then see that I could make it," his brother said.

When Dr. Stan told me that story, tears rolled down as if someone turned on a faucet. Now read this quote from Zig Ziglar: "Sometimes adversity is what you need to face in order to become successful." In the case of Dr. Stan Harris, overcoming his health situation restored his relationship with his brother as well as gave his brother faith to overcome his situation. .

There is nothing better than adversity. Every defeat, every heartbreak, every loss, contains its own seed, its own lesson on how to improve your performance the next time.
–Malcolm X

Express your Emotions and ask for Prayer!

Me: "Ashanti, can you come here please?"

Ashanti: "Here we come daddy!"

Ashanti: "Yes, daddy"

Me: "I need your help."

Ashanti: "Ok."

Me: "Daddy is struggling about writing this book. I can remember when I first wanted to write a book. I believe when this book is completed, I will feel unstoppable. I'm doing this to demonstrate that dreams do come true."

As tears started running down my face, I started affirming, "I can do this. I can do this." I looked at Ashanti and saw that she was crying too.

Ashanti: "Dad, I believe you can do it."

Me: "Thank you sweetie for believing in me."

Ashanti: "You are the best dad in the world."

Me: "Sweetie, I love you and will you pray for me?"

Ashanti: "Yes! Heavenly Father…. In Jesus name. Amen."

One powerful way to show your vulnerability is to show your emotions and to ask them to pray for you.

Don't be afraid to show your children emotions. We have been taught to not show emotions as men, but nothing can be further from the truth. I remember a conversation I had with my friend, Steve Dominguez. He said his father never told him or his siblings that he loved them. His father's logic was, "Why should I tell you I love you? I work, feed, and provide shelter for my family. That is what real love is! Anybody can say words, but if they don't show action, the words they speak are voided." Steve went ahead to say, "Now, for my children, I tell them I love them every day."

When you ask your child to pray for you, it demonstrates how you're not afraid to ask for help. Many times, as adults, our pride gets in the way to stop us from reaching for our promise.

A practical role model is a parent who inspires their children to overcome adversity by demonstrating how they overcame adversity

"The best and most beautiful things in the world cannot be seen or even touched. They must be felt with the heart." -Helen Keller

Principles

1. We have no excuse to not achieve a dream.

2. Our life is framed around five life questions:
    - Why am I here?
    - Where do I come from?
    - Who am I?
    - What can I do?
    - Where am I going?

3. Speaking life into the situation will change the situation.

4. When we overcome trials, we give power to others to overcome their test.

Prayer

Father God, in the name of Jesus, we come to You because You are teaching us how to use every resource we have to get the job done. You said in Your Word that You would never leave us nor forsake us. You already know our situation; therefore, You know how we feel. But we are going to continue to hang on to Your Word. In Jesus' name. Amen.

Questions

1. Name the excuses that have been holding you back.

2. Does your story matter to the next generation?

CHAPTER SIX

Take a Bow and Celebrate Yourself

Opportunities are like sunrises. If you wait too long, you miss them.
–William Arthur Ward

We almost DIED

It was Christmas Eve in 2014; we were in Altus, OK, eating in our favorite restaurant, Applebee. We noticed the weather starting to look very bad, so we left early to give ourselves the advantage to be safe while traveling back home.

While driving, I noticed snowflakes falling on the windshield. I looked at my wife and said, "It's starting to get bad out here." As we passed over the Pease River, entering Texas, the speed limit changed from 60 to 75 mph. At that time, my wife was talking to me about a picture on Facebook. I asked her if I could see the picture that she was referring to. When I looked at the picture, I saw a deer from the left corner of my eye. I realized it was too late! I screamed, "All shooooot!" My wife exclaimed, "What's going on!" Then BAM! The airbags deployed on impact. My airbag hit me in the chest so hard that it exploded, and air started filling up the truck.

When everyone exited the truck, my wife noticed that the passenger side windshield was spiderwebbed. The deer was killed on impact and thrown over to the upcoming traffic median.

We arrived at the emergency room, and my heart was pounding so hard that I didn't realize my pinky finger was broken. I went on Facebook, asking for prayers for my family. As I sat down, I contemplated how my family and I almost died, how fatal a moment of distraction can be, and how precious life is.

We must learn how to maximize our opportunities to live the best experience possible every day.

So, teach [us] to number our days, that we may apply [our] hearts unto wisdom.

–Psalms 90:12

So far in this book, you have learned three things: The first is how to find the WHY that will make you responsible. The second is to remember that God created you to solve a problem for Him. The third is to embrace your mentor's mentality. The fourth is to set your ideal work environment. The fifth is to employ yourself and your resources. Now, you have to TAKE A BOW AND CELEBRATE YOURSELF.

It's time to R.E.S.E.T.

Let us celebrate the occasion with wine and sweet words.
–Plautus

God Created ...

Genesis 1:1 says, "God created ..." The word 'create' means to form and to shape. It took God six days to create the universe, and on the seventh day, He rested. When God completed a specific task for each day, the Bible indicates that He said that it was good:

- Verse 4 says: "And God saw the light, that it was good: and God divided the light from the darkness."

- Verse 10 says: "God called the dry land Earth, and the gathering together of the waters called he Seas: and God saw that it was good."

- Verse 12 says: "The earth brought forth grass, and herb yielding seed after his kind, and the tree yielding fruit, whose seed was in itself, after his kind: and God saw that it was good."

- Verse 18 says: "And to rule over the day and over the night, and to divide the light from the darkness: and God saw that it was good."

- Verse 21 says: "And God created great whales and every living creature that moveth, which the waters brought forth abundantly, after their kind, and every winged fowl after his kind: and God saw that it was good."

- Verse 25 says: "God made the beast of the earth after his kind, and cattle after their kind, and everything that creepeth upon the earth after his kind: and God saw that it was good."

- Verse 31 says: "God saw everything that he had made, and, behold, it was very good. And the evening and the morning were the sixth day."

In Genesis 1:31, God said, "This is very good." Genesis 2:3 says, "And God blessed the seventh day and sanctified it: because that in it, He had rested from all His **work** which God created and made." Noticed it says that God rested from all His work? In essence, God celebrated after He finished His work. In other words, God was showing us a blueprint which tells us how He took a bow and celebrated Himself.

Performance Role Model

A performance role model is a parent who inspires their children to celebrate their achievements by demonstrating how they celebrate theirs. The last thing our children crave is having a feeling of accomplishment. As parents we must demonstrate this to them.

Just recently, my children told me that the writing of this book is a significant accomplishment, and they are very proud of me. I told them, "After the book is complete, we will celebrate!" My children saw me leave for Iraq and arrived back home. We celebrated by way of a welcome-home get together. Every time they witness me preaching in the church, we celebrate by playing video games.

I'm a VERY PROUD FATHER! My number one achievement is to see my babies walk in their PURPOSE, become PRIESTLY by following Christ, staying POSITIVE in any environment, being PRACTICAL to help someone succeed, and allowing their PERFORMANCE to give them a sense of achievement.

Our children are looking for attention, advice, admiration, affection, and feeling a since of accomplishment. We can give them more attention by becoming a Purposed Role Model. We can give them advice by becoming a Priestly Role Model. We can give them admiration by becoming a Positive Role Model. We can give them affection by becoming a Practical Role Model. We can give them feeling of accomplishment by becoming a Performance Role Model.

Every day is a New Year

One day, I asked God to teach me how to number my days, and the conversation went something like this:

God: "Everyone is looking forward to New Years to change their life because they believe they have been given a second chance to better their lives, right?"

Me: "Yes."

God: "James 4:14 says, 'You do not know what tomorrow will bring. What is your life? For you are a mist that appears for a little time and then vanishes.' Here is the problem: You don't know when it's time to check out. You have to plan for the future but maximize your today. A person can die at any moment. Most of the time, the only thing that pops up in a person's mind when death creeps up is their loved ones. They don't think about their accolades or accomplishments. Also, people will forgive one another for faults that had been committed in the past. The second thing is, when you settle in your mind that every day is a new year, you will maximize your day!"

Me: "How is every day a new year?"

God: "Simple, what is today's date?"

Me: "It's Jan 18, 2017."

God: "OK, last year Jan 18, 2016, to this year Jan 18, 2017, is a new year, right?"

Me: "Yes. I understand."

God: "Settle that in your mind right now—that every day is a new year. That is how a person can number their days."

Forgive Yourself and Others

We all live busy lives as parents. Some of us have to be SUPER PARENTS because you may be the only parent raising your child. When life gets tough, we must realize that every day, we have an opportunity to forgive ourselves and forgive our children whenever mistakes are made.

God says in Lamentations 3: 22–23, "Because of the Lord's great love we are not consumed, for his compassions never fail. They are new every morning; great is your faithfulness."

I love Apostle Paul's words: "I forget the things from which are behind and reach for those things which are before. I will press to mark for the prize of the high calling of God in Christ Jesus. I can't change for where I have been, but I can change for where I'm going. I will make up my mind that I will go anywhere but backward" (Philippians 3:13 [paraphrased]).

Forgiveness is the key for people to continue to move into their greatness. I forgave my father for not being there for me. I forgave my mother for not being there for specific critical functions in my life. I had to forgive myself for not doing certain things as a parent. I know there will be many mistakes my daughters will make, but I must have a forgiving heart and give them support to help them correct the error.

When you forgive, you in no way change the past—but you sure do change the future.
–Bernard Meltzer

Put a Name on Every Moment

To not miss any opportunities in your day, you must give every moment a name by living your day on purpose. How? You must schedule it! You must plan time to grind! You must schedule time with family. You must make time for yourself.

When we do have the time to be with our children, we must be FULLY PRESENT with them. We must put our cell phones down and have a conversation with our children. Make a rule in your house that all phones will be off while eating dinner or watching a movie. If your child isn't hungry, tell them to sit at the table while the others eat. Start a conversation by saying, "How was everyone's day?" Share your experience first to open a dialogue. Share a joke or something that will break the ice. When it's just my daughters and me in the house, I make them put their phones up and come into the living room with me to talk about life.

Social media can be a curse, but it is also a blessing. Facebook, Instagram, and many other platforms can give you the ability to capture great moments. I like the fact that you can also see other people's great moments ... Pictures and videos give you the ability to put a name on every moment.

In the remaining part of this chapter, I want you to celebrate with my family on the things my daughters have achieved and how I was able to complete this book. The stories I'm going to present to you bring tears to my eyes as I type this sentence.

A Call from the School

My wife, Ladonna, called me and said, "Willie, I got a call at work today. When I saw the number, it was one that I didn't recognize. Usually, I don't answer unfamiliar numbers, but this day, something was different. Maybe I was in a good mood. So, I went ahead and answered it. It happened to be one of the kids' teachers. She said, 'Is this Mrs. Tubbs?' I answered, 'Yes, it is!' She began by saying, 'I'm calling to let you know that I have had the privilege of teaching both of your girls. They were very mannerable and a pure joy to have in my class. You and your husband truly have something to be proud of. I can tell you both are doing an awesome job of raising your daughters. Thank you for sharing your wonderful children with me.'"

The Bet

In September 2017, I told my daughter Vatanie, "If you make a 95 or above on your report card, I will give you 100 dollars." She said "Great!" because she needed a laptop computer. In November, she walked toward me and said, "Here is my report card." I glanced at the report card and said, "Sweetie, great job," and I hugged her. Some people may say I'm raising her to be motivated by money, but I say that her PURPOSE motivates her!

Former President Barack Obama said something very profound, and I know it will bless you. He said, "Money is not the only answer, but it makes a difference." So, I said to my daughter, "Great job, Vatanie! I love you and thank you for reminding me that a person has to RUN AFTER THEIR DESTINY to achieve the desired outcome." #proudfather

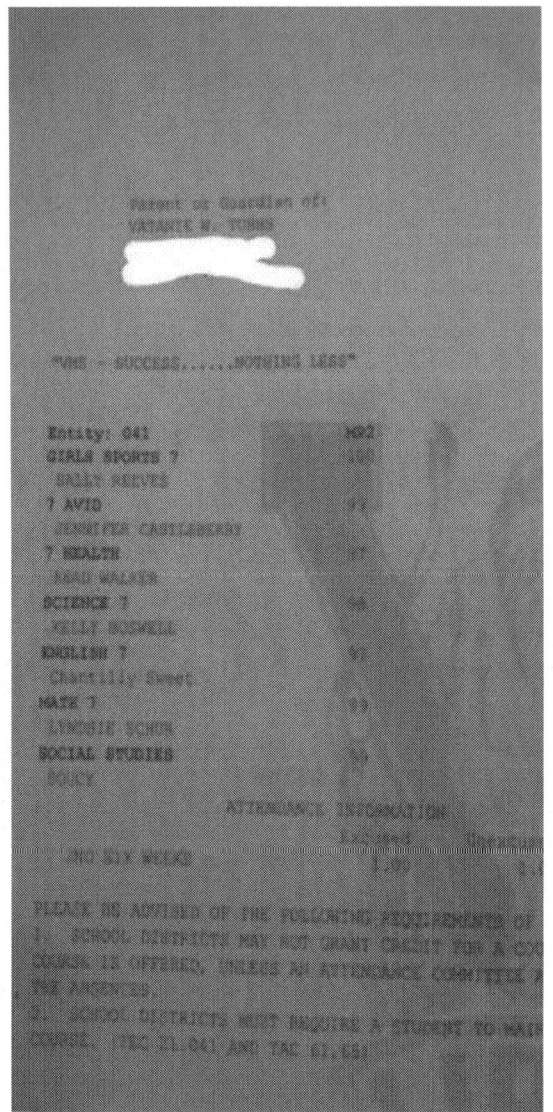

UIL

"Hello, this is Willie Tubbs."

"Daddy, this is Ashanti."

"Hey, sweetie, how are you?"

"Daddy, you won't believe what place I got in UIL!"

"What place did you get, sweetie?"

"I got first place in Art Appreciation!"

"YOU GOT FIRST! Oh my God! Tell me what you

want, and Daddy will buy it for you!"

"OK, Daddy, I will let you know."

"Sweetie, I'm so proud of you!"

"Thank you, Daddy!" Ashanti said.

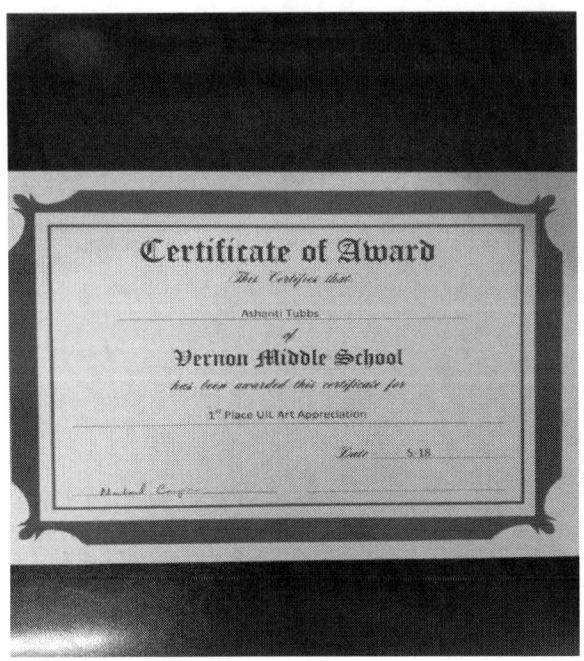

I low was I able to complete this book?
One word: LOVE

A performance role model is a parent who inspires their children to celebrate their achievements by demonstrating how they celebrate their own achievements.

Parents, it's time to R.E.S.E.T.

Live so that when your children think of fairness, caring, and integrity, they think of you.
–H. Jackson Brown, Jr.

Principles

1. Our life is like a mist that appears for a little while.

2. Every day is a new year.

3. Without forgiveness, you cannot maximize your day!

4. Your children are looking for attention, advice, affection, and admiration.

5. Every moment has a name.

Prayer

Father God, in the name of Jesus, we pray from this day on that we will maximize our day. Father, teach us to forgive ourselves and others. As You have given us children to raise, help us to be fully present for our children, and Father, our goal is to break the generational curse off this world. We are world-class, Father. In Jesus' name. Amen.

Questions

1. What can you change right now to maximize your time with your children?

2. How important is it to be fully present with your Children?

3. Who do you have to forgive in order to maximize your day?

4. How important is it for you to make a decision to change the course of your family's future?

In Conclusion

Get M.A.D.

Former World Heavyweight Boxing Champion James 'Bonecrusher' Smith wrote a book, titled *M.A.D.*, describing a one-step system he used to seize every moment to win in life. The book title exemplifies the method he used: M.A.D. (Make A Decision). With his one-step philosophy, he became the first world heavyweight champion with a college degree. I had an opportunity to do business with him.

One day, Bonecrusher told me a story of how he sued Don King for breach of contract. He said that Don promised him the opportunity to fight a world title fight but didn't deliver on his promise. One day, Don King called Bonecrusher, and the conversation went something like this:

Don King: "Bonecrusher, I want to settle this lawsuit with you. I'm going to give you that title fight!"

Bonecrusher: "Oh, really? With who? Where is it going to be? When is it going to happen?"

Don King: "With the person that beat you last year. Tim Witherspoon."

Bonecrusher: "When is the fight supposed to happen and where?"

Don King: "The fight will be held at Madison Square Garden."

Bonecrusher: "When is the fight supposed to happen?"

Don King: "The fight will be on HBO. Bonecrusher, you have an opportunity to redeem yourself in front of the whole world."

Bonecrusher: "Don, when is this fight?"

Don King: "It will be next week."

Bonecrusher: "Don, you mean to tell me I have only seven days to prepare to fight a guy that beat me last year?"

Don King: "Yes, take it or leave it!"

Bonecrusher: "Yes, I will take the fight because I have a dream that one day, I will be sharing this story to inspire people."

To make a long story short, at the beginning of the fight, James 'Bonecrusher' Smith said he got M.A.D. and knocked down Tim Witherspoon three times in the first round and ended the fight. He credited his boxing career to his M.A.D philosophy.

He had 60 professional fights in his 18-year career. His record was 44 wins, 17 losses, and one draw. 32 of the wins were KO. He had several successful network marketing businesses—and not to forget that he was ordained in 1997.

Why tell James 'Bonecrusher' Smith's story? I love his M.A.D. philosophy because you must Make A Decision to knock out debt by focusing on financial freedom. You must Make A Decision to knock out the negative environment by focusing on a positive environment. You must Make A Decision to knock out your lousy character by focusing on Christ who has given you your true identity. You must Make A Decision to knock out adversity by focusing on the promises of God. You must Make A Decision to knock out doubt by focusing on your capabilities. You must Make A Decision to knock out this generational curse by leading your children to their greatness!

I'm pissed off for greatness. Because if you ain't pissed off for greatness, that means you're OK with being mediocre.
–Ray Lewis

I H.O.P.E.(Help Other People Excel) my testimony has helped you believe that you can rescue yourself and lead your children to their GREATNESS.

LET'S GO TO WORK!

THANK YOU

Special thanks to the following individuals for believing in my dream before it even came to pass:

1. Josh Rogers
2. Alicia Bear
3. Charles MacArthur
4. Ladonna Tubbs
5. Gregory Mullen
6. Ulyssia Straughter
7. Dr. Stan and Nadia Harris
8. Frederick Anderson
9. Bette Laughrun
10. Stephanie Stewart
11. Deidra Reece
12. Mike Slayton
13. Torrey Dennis
14. Naona Nichole Eldridge
15. Adele J. Foster-Glenn
16. Shawnda Maxwell

17. Tyler Gray
18. Nichole Brawmer
19. Darlene Howard
20. Emiliano Canchola
21. Abimbola Adalumo
22. Jerry Tubbs
23. Chante Kelly
24. Stevie McGregor
25. Chrishelle Mckenzie
26. La'Donna Davis
27. Ray Wiley
28. Nitosha Tubbs
29. Tony Rogers Jr.
30. Jennifer Wilkinson
31. Linda Diaz
32. Marsha Cowell
33. Sharon Favors
34. Wendy Morgan
35. Brenda Johnson
36. Andre Roy
37. Nikki Hall
38. Susan Wilson
39. Dean Renfro
40. Tyrone and Terracia Campbell
41. Jen Butler

42. Steve Stucke
43. Lem Moore
44. Janelle Montgomery
45. Amber N. Mejia
46. Satandra Gates
47. William Simpson
48. April Grant
49. Chloé Dawson
50. Dale & Josie Donnell
51. Brandi Murphy
52. Ray Brooks

www.agentsofchangeLLC.com

Made in the USA
Lexington, KY
02 November 2019

56412604R00087